Testim

Catherine Carrigan has done it again -- pulled together a wealth of material from her own deep experiential wisdom. This time she helps us find the soul inside ordinary experiences, especially the seemingly negative ones. It's so important that we learn to see through our challenges and fear to the compassionate revelation of the soul's sanity within. It's part of remembering who we really are. It's part of becoming transparent. You'll find tremendous reassurance and guidance in this book.

- Penney Peirce, Author of *Transparency Leap of Perception,* and *Frequency*

Catherine Carrigan is an unequaled master of reading the soul. This is her greatest gift, and the work she has come here to do. As she shares not only her stories, but her technique, you may find your own soul responding to the love she has poured into every page. And when you have finished reading it, you may find that you have changed.

- Maxine Taylor
  America's First Licensed Astrologer, Author of
  Move Into the Magic

If you have never heard of medical intuitives and what they are actually capable of, this book is the key to unlock that mystery. Catherine reaches deep into her toolbox on this book and reveals her magical way of working with great precedent. This book brings all of her skills to the surface as she reveals what true healing represents. I believe her methods and teachings are a paradigm we should all embrace for a better future. I believe Catherine to be a true shaman if you will as she can see deep into a person's being and bring everything to the surface so they may simply heal themselves. To me she is the living version of the great Edgar Cayce!

- Darin McBratney, Owner of Costa Rica Yoga Spa and Iboga Therapy

What an honor and a privilege! When Catherine invited me to write an endorsement for her new book *Reading the Soul*, I was both delighted and thrilled. Three pages into the book … and I was moved to tears. The story reached my heart and touched my soul. I instantly recognized in the person described someone I love dearly -- awakening a profound desire for them to be healed in the same way. I ploughed ahead, eagerly devouring story after riveting story -- an astonishing and enlightening collection of healing journeys.

I soon realized that my endorsement was secondary to the blessing of this book touching my life. At the time of reading, my world was in turmoil -- in the throes of moving house and a life in chaos. God, the Universe, or whatever you believe, surely knew that I would not have taken the time to read this book. It's clear that Catherine was guided to send me this book -- enabling me to be the beneficiary of this profound knowledge -- healing my soul and connect to its true purpose.

One of life's biggest lessons is to learn to love ourselves, thus allowing others to love us in turn. Catherine generously shares her remarkable and profound knowledge -- leading us to understand how we can connect to our true selves -- pursue and achieve our soul's divine purpose with ease and joy … simply by being ourselves. Catherine demands that we relinquish the urge to find the answers. She advocates we reject intellectual understanding. Instead, we must open ourselves up to direct experience with the divine.

If you yearn for a soul-connected life, then 'Reading the Soul' is a must-read. An outstanding lesson on how to let go and let our souls show us the way.

- Olivia Beardsmore, Founder of Burning Woman

Catherine Carrigan's new book, *Reading the Soul,* gets right to the heart of matters.

Beyond overview, case studies, holistic understanding and intuitive wisdom, this book offers a true template for understanding and assisting ourselves and others in the sacred work of soul evolution. Use this book to wake up, align, clear and live a soul-driven, purposeful life of fulfillment and service to all Being.

- Gabriela Masala, Transformational Consultant, Facilitator, Evolutionary Soul

In *Reading the Soul*, Catherine Carrigan gracefully shares many healing stories from her clients to demonstrate how medical intuitives work and what they can do to help you heal. As a healer myself, I find work like hers invaluable!

All wounds are experienced physically in the body, mental mentally in the mind, and spiritually in the heart! It is my opinion, and personal experience, that consulting with someone as skilled as Catherine is a requirement when it comes to healing that can help you to heal on each of these levels and is sustainable, deep, and long-lasting. This book acts as an opening for anyone interested in learning what a medical intuitive is, how this skill can help them to heal, and why consulting a medical intuitive is important.

Reading the Soul can open your heart and mind and facilitate your own personal healing.

- Peter Bedard, MA, C.Ht., Author, *Convergence Healing: Healing Pain with Energetic Love*

Catherine is an earthly angel who lives her gifts. This book *Reading the Soul* is an easy read and explains how she works with her spiritual connection to help healing on the soul level. How to live with spirit guides, angels and archangels is clearly explained for those who want to work with spirit to heal. If you are searching, this book is a must read."

- Rachel Shackleton, Medical Herbalist (DipHerb), Naturopath (DipNat), Kinesiologist (DipK), Fresh Air Fridays Facilitator

Reading the Soul captures the essence of what all spiritual knowledge is based upon. Catherine gives a clear understanding of your soul's purpose and the different soul contracts you chose before you incarnated. She fills the holes and questions that most people have about why certain things are happening in their life. *Reading the Soul* is insightful, uplifting and inspiring!

- Meghan Olsgard, Spiritual Life Coach at Infinite Soul Blueprint

Have you ever struggled to understand why your life is the way it is? Perhaps there is a recurring pattern that just seems to elude your awareness? *Reading the Soul* takes a deep dive into the many ways we can fall out of grace with our own soul. Catherine Carrigan brings vast intuitive insights about the not-so-obvious ways we can struggle in life. Each topic brings a story with it to back it up with a real-life example. This book offers a comprehensive review of the many ways we can get stuck in our own journey, so that we can ultimately evolve from these experiences. Take the deep dive into your own soul's journey by immersing yourself in *Reading the Soul*.

- Les Jensen, Radio Host, Inspirational Speaker and Coach, and Author of *Citizen King: The New Age of Power, Forgiven Sinner: God's Last Savior,* and *Personal Power Fundamentals*.

Catherine Carrigan's book, *Reading the Soul*, brings us a critical message: "If you want to understand and control your health, you MUST learn to communicate with your soul." In a world with a broken healthcare system, in a world where big companies profit off of our addictions, insecurities and disease, in a world where people are craving connection and don't know how to get it, Catherine's book not only give us a guide, but also the stories and examples necessary to adopt and integrate a whole new way to look at the reality we experience.

- Ani Anderson, CEO of NEW Health Inc., bestselling author of *Find Your Soul's Agenda*

Catherine Carrigan's latest book, *Reading the Soul*, is both a delightful read and a great resource for soul connection. She uses stories and anecdotes to illustrate the many ways in which we all can understand and heal our soul. She even provides step-by-step instruction on healing techniques that any reader can use to feel less burdened and more energized right away. In *Reading the Soul*, Catherine has once again gifted readers with a clear grasp of healing and the power of love.

- Nina Lynn, author of *You're the One* and *Gracie and Sammy*

Self-love is key and in her latest book, Catherine Carrigan shows how important it is to draw on this internal well rather than looking to the outer world for fulfillment. As always, her insights are deep and on point, and she explores the blocks to love and how to release them.

- Jean Adrienne, author and developer of InnerSpeak™

Catherine Carrigan's newest book *Reading the Soul* gives the reader a thorough explanation of the high-quality healing works she provides. This captivating, detailed book provides insight to the reader about all the reasons we get sick, struggle with life and our relationships, are unhappy or live in fear. Catherine shows her expertise as she explains how healing works and gives the reader specific prayers, activities and areas to consider in their quest for healing. On top of all that, the client examples that she has personally facilitated make for fascinating, can't-put-the-book-down reading.

- Lynne Cockrum-Murphy, Ed.D., L.I.S.A.C., Theta Healer, Spiritual Teacher, Speaker, Author

Catherine has written a compelling story-based look into *Reading the Soul.* As a transformational shaman and healer who has studied for 40 years, there is rarely a book that teaches me something new. But this book has done that, and in such a wonderfully written way that I found it hard to put down.

- Kelle Sparta, The Spirit Doctor (TM)

In Catherine's new book, I was constantly fascinated by the depth and scope of her knowledge and wisdom about our soul journeys. There's great richness in the stories she presents that give us better insight into the many aspects of our soul contracts and karmic wounds we are here to work through. The book also illustrates her profound intuitive awareness that has helped so many people.

- Peter Roth, Medical Intuitive Healer, Author, Human Design analyst

Catherine Carrigan is an angel who talks to angels. In *Reading the Soul* she pulls back the curtain to let us know how such a conversation might go. It's not limited to the four-dimensional spacetime language we share. She writes with the confidence and clarity of one familiar with that uncertain world, guided by love and service. All true healing restores Wholeness and Integrity to the Soul, and through many real life examples she points out the soul-traps that disrupt it. She takes the reader by the hand and reminds you of the beauty of your authentic Self.

- Rick Barrett, Author of *Finding You in a World of It* and *Taijiquan: Through the Western Gate*

Reading the Soul

by Catherine Carrigan

Book design by RamaJon
Cover design by RamaJon

Available for order through Ingram Press Catalogues

Catherine Carrigan

Visit my websites at

www.catherinecarrigan.com
www.unlimitedenergynow.com

Printed in the United States of America

First Printing: October 2019

ISBN: 978-0-9894506-6-9

TABLE OF CONTENTS

Book I
Love Opens the Impossible

"I am not afraid. I was born to do this."
- Joan of Arc

Chapter 1:
The Actor Who Thought He Was Unlovable

"Knowing that we can be loved exactly as we are gives us all the best opportunity for growing into the healthiest of people."

- *Fred Rogers*

Everybody thinks that if only they were rich and famous, life would be so easy.

As if!

Enter stage left: Bobby (not his real name), star of Hollywood movies and countless TV shows, was universally loved. Trouble was, Bobby, the actual person, did not love himself.

I first conducted a medical intuitive reading for Bobby before he attended a healing retreat for much-needed inner reflection.

"You are still working on clearing your karma of addiction," I wrote to Bobby.

"Recognize that it's part of your personality to suffer from addiction.

"You can even be an addiction for others – what I mean is that other people can become addicted to you, your personality and your aura.

"It's easy for you to get hooked on substances, e.g., coffee, marijuana, tobacco and other substances, so observe yourself. I believe as you become more deeply connected to your true self, you will have less need for outside substances to feel stimulated.

"Affirming 'I am enough, I have enough, I do enough' would be a good message for you. Remember that more is not always better."

After I started writing the rough draft of this book, I didn't give Bobby another thought until a few weeks later when I received a call from the healing center's director.

"I've never seen this before," the director told me. "Usually everybody gets better."

Even though Bobby had benefited from acupuncture, fresh air, organic food and plant medicine, upon returning back to real life, the self-hatred he had been trying to push away reared its ugly head, and he started drinking uncontrollably.

He spoke with me by phone from as he was trying to learn the lines for a new movie.

"I rebelled after I was told I was adopted," Bobby admitted.

"I sabotaged my career for 10 years. I really felt undeserving, so I would blow it.

"I've been blowing it for years."

The only thing Bobby knew how to do was to act.

In fact, he was such a skilled performer he had been acting his way through real life, pretending to be who he thought everybody else wanted him to be.

Acting had first become a survival skill and then his chosen profession.

Bobby was so good at it he found himself costarring with A-listers and pretending to be the hero his soul actually longed to be.

When I conducted his original medical intuitive reading, I explained he had lost certain fragments of his soul: "I believe you have lost who you were before you became an actor.

"Being with people who don't know who you are professionally is highly beneficial for you as there is no need to play a role other than your true self.

"You don't believe anybody can love you for who you really are, so when people get too close, you push them away."

I explained to Bobby that although he might have thought of himself as abandoned, in fact, his soul had a unique path to being born.

Often when a baby is conceived, the pregnancy doesn't work out (and not necessarily because of an abortion).

Sometimes, through no fault of the mother or the baby, the pregnancy fails, and the little soul who was trying to be born has to find another set of birth parents.

A soul may try one set of birth parents after another until a pregnancy actually succeeds.

Bobby's birth parents, I explained to him, were in fact his eleventh try. His birth mother had a soul agreement to help him to be born.

"When you try multiple times to be born, you have a very important purpose for being here," I explained. "It's as if you're trying to get to a certain place by a certain time. When the first train doesn't work out, you take what you can get.

"Your birth mother was your soul friend. She helped you get born."

The parents who adopted Bobby loved him very much. He felt guilty about how often he had tested them.

Meanwhile, their love for him remained unshakeable.

As he sat in a cafe trying to digest the lines for his new movie, I began a healing for him so he would understand he is lovable.

“One of your big life lessons is to learn how to love your true self and to allow other people to love you.

“Because you truly believe that the real you isn’t lovable, you tend to test people. This affects your care -- also -- the more you can allow others to love you, the more successful you will be in your work.

“You keep the energy of love outside of yourself. You don’t let it in -- it's always on the outside.

“That’s a lonely place to be.”

When we came to the part of the healing where he would need to forgive himself, I asked him to repeat the simple line, “I forgive Bobby.”

Tears welled in his eyes.

Even though worldwide audiences had hung on every line Bobby spoke in his movies, he just couldn’t even mouth the words.

“I will say the mantra for you,” I offered.

I asked Bobby to put his hand over his heart so he could receive the forgiveness where he needed it most.

“I FORGIVE BOBBY.
BOBBY FORGIVES ME.
I LOVE BOBBY.
BOBBY LOVES ME,”

I affirmed.

For a moment, Bobby was no longer acting.

There were real tears -- emotions that came from the depths of his soul. He felt the sadness that had been welling up inside him for more than 50 years.

I continued with the words of Ho'oponopono, the ancient Hawaiian forgiveness mantra:

"I'M SORRY, BOBBY.
PLEASE FORGIVE ME, BOBBY.
I LOVE YOU, BOBBY.
THANK YOU, BOBBY."

His soul was grieving

It had been exhausting -- all those years of pretending and all the time lost from keeping everybody on the outside and not letting in the love his soul craved.

Chapter 2:
The Healer Who Constantly Washed Her Hands

"By surrendering, you create an energy field of receptivity for the solution to appear."

- Wayne Dyer

Jan (not her real name) was a sought-after teacher of kinesiology and belief clearing. She maintained a full practice and helped many clients overcome depression, anxiety and a multitude of other challenges.

Despite her ability to heal others, Jan felt deeply ashamed. She had developed a terrible case of obsessive-compulsive disorder (OCD) that manifested in constant hand washing.

Jan would arrive at my healing room with little plastic baggies of tissues so she could wipe her hands clean. Afterwards, she would hide the baggies in the bushes around my garden, apparently not realizing I would eventually find them.

Even though Jan had consulted shamans, medical doctors, kinesiologists, naturopaths and a wide range of other traditional and alternative healers, no one had been able to identify or clear the true source of her struggle.

Jan had closely examined her own beliefs but couldn't figure out why she continued to struggle with OCD. She felt ashamed she couldn't clear the problem herself.

As I began to do healing work with Jan, I explained that she had a huge hole in her energy field.

It's a law of physics that anytime an electrical current runs vertically, there is a magnetic field surrounding it. In the human body, that equates to your personal energy field. New age healers call it your aura.

"You have a large hole in your field," I told Jan.

The hole was literally as large as her back, extending from shoulder to shoulder and down to her hip bone.

Just as your skin serves as a covering for your internal organs, connective tissue and bones, your energy field provides a layer of protection for your soul. Whenever you have a hole in your field, you become hypersensitive.

Noise, electromagnetic frequencies, other people's emotions, geopathic stress and a wide range of other energetic shifts can disturb your well-being.

It was as if her soul was being rubbed raw.

It was as if her soul constantly felt dirty with all the energy she was unknowingly picking up.

The only way Jan could comfort herself, to try to clean herself, was by constantly washing her hands.

I was able to clear the energetic attachments that had settled into her damaged aura and sealed her energy field.

At last, Jan's hand washing ended!

It wasn't a matter of discussing her childhood traumas, having a more positive attitude or taking a pill. After her energy field was healed, her soul could finally feel calm again, and she no longer needed to wash her hands.

Chapter 3:
The Indigo Child in the Ivory Tower

"Loneliness and the feeling of being unwanted is the most terrible poverty."

- Mother Theresa

Amal (not her real name) lived with her mother in a high-rise apartment in one of the wealthiest cities in the world, where the average citizen enjoyed a net worth exceeding $17 million.

After I did a medical intuitive reading for her brother, he asked me to do a reading for Amal. At the age of 36, she was unmarried, had few friends and did not seem to fit in anywhere.

Her family loved Amal, but nobody really knew how to help her.

As we worked through the medical intuitive reading, I could see Amal was suffering from a lack of brain integration. Although people typically have a dominant eye, her brain had not fully developed, and her eye dominance had not been established.

The ensuing neurological confusion led to constant turmoil in Amal's nervous system, which caused her to feel severely exhausted.

Despite the brain integration challenges, however, I saw

Amal was a very sensitive little soul. During the reading, I explained that she is an indigo child, one of a group of psychically perceptive souls who came to the planet to be of service by uplifting others.

During the late 1970s, many children were born with indigo, a deep purplish blue, in their auras.

Indigo children are sometimes diagnosed with learning disabilities while at the same time being highly intelligent, off-the-charts intuitive, compassionately empathic and very caring.

"One of the things that is holding you back is a lack of purpose in your life," I wrote to Amal. "When I ask my guides about your higher spiritual purpose, I am being told that you are to use your innate sensitivity for plant communication."

Amal was living in the high-rise apartment, literally ungrounded from the earth and away from the trees, shrubs and flowers her soul longed to enjoy.

"Your soul may receive great benefit from tending plants.

"Although I know you crave human companionship, I believe you will find it most easily when you find other indigo children like yourself.

"Even though you are close to your family and love them and they love you, you will do even better when you find your soul tribe."

No matter who you are -- no matter how special you may be -- your soul needs the comfort and companionship of people just like you.

Amal didn't fit in because she didn't know other people exactly like her. She just needed to understand whom to go look for -- other spiritually directed, psychic, independent souls wanting to raise the consciousness of the planet!

Chapter 4:
Not Exactly the Soul Mate She Was Looking For

"Dare to declare who you are. It is not far from the shores of silence to the boundaries of speech. The path is not long, but the way is deep. You must not only walk there, you must be prepared to leap."

- *Hildegard Von Bingen*

Laura (not her real name) was wearing a long dress and a wide-brimmed hat when she showed up at a Kentucky Derby party. Newly divorced, she was feeling fully alive again when she happened to meet James (also not his real name).

After the first few days of instant attraction and nonstop conversation, James admitted he was married and had two kids. He assured Laura, however, that his marriage wasn't happy and he spent most of his life on the road for work.

Although the affair fell completely outside Laura's ethical boundaries, she couldn't stop loving James. They communicated every day for hours and hours, both by phone and instant messages, revealing truths about themselves they had never shared with anyone.

James helped Laura secure a position in his company where she could earn a salary large enough to support herself and her two children. On company trips, they spent time together, as James always promised he was soon going to muster the courage to reveal everything to his wife back home.

Up to that point, Laura's definition of a soul mate had been a man who was her true match on every level. Indeed, James met that description: handsome, highly educated, insightful and witty.

But what Laura hadn't bargained for was the truth of what a soul mate actually is.

Your soul mate is any person whose soul forces your soul to grow. Soul friends have contracts with you to face the truth about yourself in ways you might never have anticipated.

Every time Laura and James were together, they experienced a happiness she had never known. Her secret weekends with him, however, were followed by catastrophic depressions so severe it took weeks for her to get back to feeling semi-normal again.

Without judgment, I explained that every time Laura came away from James, knowing he was returning to his wife and children, was essentially the same as recovering from open-heart surgery.

Laura's heart would open, then break, and open and break again and again and again.

Laura thought her divorce had been the hardest trial she had ever been through. But nothing, she reported to me, was as difficult for her as loving a man who would not be true to her.

“He’s addicted to his ego facade,” I explained to Laura. “He simply cannot face himself.”

Finally, after three and a half years, Laura broke off all communication.

Although she had been married before and deeply loved her children, Laura’s heart had never been fully open until she met James.

As Laura gathered the strength to say goodbye, she grounded herself in her soul integrity in a way she had never known.

She came in one day to see me.

“I think I am a depressed person,” she announced.

As I had known her a very long time, I demurred.

“I would change my language on that,” I advised her.

“Instead of labeling yourself a depressed person, just realize that you have never learned how to be happy.”

As we worked together, we identified what her soul longed for.

“This is not a Prozac deficiency,” I observed.

“You have made so many other priorities in life your goals -- having children, making a living. Now it’s time to give yourself permission to be truly happy.”

As Laura focused on her own soul longing, the priorities in her life began to shift. More than anything, she realized the one person who needed to love her was herself.

Laura gave herself permission to love herself enough to become a happy person.

Chapter 5:
The Exhausted CEO

"When we experience Soul Loss, we begin experiencing feelings of weakness, fatigue, depression, anxiety and emptiness. We just know that something is missing from our lives, but we don't know what."

- Mateo Sol

William (not his real name), chief executive officer of a privately held company started a generation ago by his father, was always telling me how tired he felt. When he first began working with me, he suffered from pain and exhaustion.

We got rid of the pain in William's pelvis and back rather quickly, but the exhaustion persisted. In fact, he told me so often how tired he felt, I even wrote a book, *Unlimited Energy Now,* to help him get over his chronic fatigue.

William learned how to improve his diet and quickly adapted to the practices of Reiki and qi gong.

I could honestly say his all-organic diet was better than mine: smoothies every morning and no sugar, alcohol, or gluten. He was so disciplined he never slipped up.

William would visit the very best doctors in the U.K.

After running the latest round of up-to-the minute health assessments, they would report back to him, "Son, you are the healthiest person we have seen all year."

Still, William remain unconvinced. He felt there had to be a physical cause for his exhaustion.

William would call me for appointments every six months or so on Skype. Although his emotions were sometimes different, my answer was always the same: "It's emotional."

During that time, William came to realize he wasn't actually in love with his wife. Although they had a wonderful friendship, the passionate connection he longed for had never existed.

They plodded through life together raising their son until one day William announced he couldn't take it any longer. He confessed to me he had been hanging onto the marriage for the sake of his son, Buddy.

William's parents had divorced when he was a young teen, and he didn't want Buddy growing up the way he had, as the only child of a divorced mother.

After years of working through the details, William and his wife finally separated. He moved to another part of the country, to be closer to London for his growing business.

Every other weekend, Buddy would come to stay with William and his new partner. During the week, however, he would long for his son so much that outside of his job he could think of virtually nothing else.

William was constantly sending messages asking me about the latest amino acid formulations, still hoping to find the solution to his fatigue in natural supplements. Indeed, they made enough of a difference that he began lifting weights at a gym several times a week.

William's body looked ripped, but the deep, heavy fatigue remained. After years of taking the amino acids, he set up another appointment with me.

"Even though Buddy is still young (at that point, he was 12 years old), he is your soul mate," I explained to William. "Throughout your life, you will be closer to Buddy than any other person -- man or woman.

"You are tired because your soul is aching, you are missing Buddy so terribly."

William told me that Buddy had already declared his ambition to work in the family business someday.

"He is too young to understand this whole soul mate thing. But the two of you really need each other," I said.

By then, William's relationship with his ex-wife had become so friendly that he was able to convince her to let Buddy spend more time at his new home. The ex needed more time to herself to exercise, begin dating again and rest after the long weeks of working full-time while raising her only son.

As Buddy began to spend more time at his new home, William noticed his own energy level beginning to soar again. His soul fulfilled, his boy beside him, the exhaustion began to wane.

Chapter 6: Why Natural Healing Isn't All Just Celery Juice and Yoga

"All disease has a mental correspondence, and in order to heal the body one must first 'heal the soul.'"
- *Florence Scovel Shinn*

In my work as a medical intuitive healer, I take a broad view of health.

You are a soul who has a body.

Your soul controls your mind.

Your mind controls your emotions.

Your emotions control your energy.

And finally, last but not least, your energy controls your physical body.

Most people think of health as consisting primarily of what goes on with your physical body. If you think that way, you aren't exactly wrong.

If you want to experience radiant health, however, you must understand how the five levels of your being interpenetrate, control and affect one another. You must consider those other aspects of who you actually are.

The most powerful level on which to work is your soul level because it controls all the other levels.

That's why I have written *Reading the Soul.*

If you were to visit a medical doctor, she might order bloodwork, listen to your organs through a stethoscope or order an MRI, X-ray or other diagnostic test.

A naturopath might read your organs through your acupuncture system.

An acupuncturist might take your pulse to read your meridians.

A psychologist might ask you about your childhood or question what's going on with your work or family life.

A life coach might ask what motivates you, what your goals are and in what direction you hope to lead your life. A rabbi, imam or priest might ask you about your prayer life or what spiritual texts you've been reading.

All of the above approaches might give a glimpse of your total well-being.

I believe you must address all five levels–of yourself -- your physical, energetic, emotional, mental and spiritual bodies. When you dig in, determine the issues to be resolved and put together a blueprint for their resolution, you can supercharge your healing and experience profound personal transformation.

There are advanced systems for reading your physical, energetic, emotional and mental bodies. Until now, however, we've had no system for assessing what's going on with you at the soul level.

What could be more indescribable than your soul?

You may know your blood pressure or have an idea about your height or weight. An energy healer may have read your chakras. And even if you don't have words, a kinesiologist can easily read the emotions you've been grappling with.

But what's your soul doing? How does it communicate with your ego mind?

In what way does your soul guide you?

For what purposes were you born?

What wounds does your soul carry forward from your current or any other lifetime?

Have you managed to get your shadow out of way enough to listen?

Are there negative spiritual energies holding you back from reaching your pure soul potential?

What karma has your soul yet to resolve?

These are the questions I do my best to answer when I am reading your soul.

Chapter 7:
What Is a Medical Intuitive Reading?

"You ought not to heal the body without the soul, for this is the great error of our day in treating the human body."
- Plato

Here is the template I use when I'm engaged in a medical intuitive reading.

Medical Intuitive Reading

AGE:

OVERALL CHI LEVEL (50/100 would be average for a man or woman your age):

MOST STRESSED ORGAN (72 to 85 percent is normal healthy functioning for an organ -- higher isn't better as you don't want your organs to overwork):

PHYSICAL:
ENERGETIC:
EMOTIONAL:
MENTAL:
SPIRITUAL:
ENVIRONMENT:
NUTRITION:
SUPPLEMENTS:
SUPPORTIVE THERAPIES:
EXERCISE:

I begin by reading what I see is happening on the five levels of your being:

PHYSICAL. This would include identifying imbalances in organs and organ systems and looking for parasites, bad bacteria and viral infections as well as other disease processes.

ENERGETIC. This includes examining how well grounded you are into your physical body. I look at whether your major chakras are open or closed. I focus on the five flows of your breath -- the inhale, exhale, breath around your belly, breath around your head and breath from your navel out into your arms, legs and head. I also review the balance of your acupuncture system and whether there are any holes or tears in your energy field.

EMOTIONAL. I zero in on the primary emotion or emotions that are occupying your mind.

MENTAL. What thoughts and beliefs are holding you back? I can look at your level of brain integration, which is how well the right and left hemispheres are working together. I also determine if your ego is getting in the way of your soul growth and whether your shadow is ruining your life.

SPIRITUAL. Are you suffering from any soul wounds? I can dig deeper into your soul purpose, find out where you are along your soul path, uncover your soul longing, expose any karma that you have not finished processing and reveal whether any negative spiritual energies are attached to you.

After exploring the five levels of your being, I make specific recommendations:

ENVIRONMENT. What kind of environment do you need to thrive? We often forget our environment is the most powerful factor in our health. Is your home conducive to your well-being? Does your office support your health?

NUTRITION. We'll discuss what, when and how you eat. I may recommend certain foods to avoid and others that will support your body. Diets are highly individual and depend on your body type as well as the health of your metabolism. There are so many diets out there, but which one will be the most supportive for your body at this time?

SUPPLEMENTS. These would include natural healing remedies, vitamins, minerals, herbs, digestive aids, amino acids and homeopathy. As I am not a medical doctor, I don't comment on medications but do make specific recommendations about natural approaches.

SUPPORTIVE THERAPIES. We can discuss a wide range of holistic approaches including acupuncture, Reiki, craniosacral therapy, detoxification programs, far infrared sauna, lifestyle coaching, massage, physical therapy and more.

EXERCISE. Your physical body is part of your animal nature. Just as different diets work better for different people, some forms of exercise may bring balance to your body while other approaches may deplete you. We can discuss walking in nature, tai chi, qi gong, yoga, weight training, swimming, surfing, martial arts, interval training, cycling, running or other forms of exercise. Exercise may also include activities for your brain and eyes.

A medical intuitive reading can lead to great insights into what's going on with you and provide a blueprint for optimal health.

Chapter 8:
What Is a Soul Reading?

"It is impossible to heal the body without healing the soul."

- Socrates

A soul reading empowers you to understand what is going on with yourself on the soul level.

There are three stages in your soul path:

Unconscious. In the early stages of your spiritual development, you may not be aware of yourself as a soul or be conscious of what it is really up to in this lifetime.

Awakening. You discover that you are in fact a soul and are in the process of waking up to your soul purpose.

Conscious. You have discovered your soul purpose and are taking action to fulfill it.

Karma Clearing To-Do List

While marching down your soul path, you may be digging up soul baggage, soul suffering or past life patterns that can be cleared through deep healing work.

This world is truly the field of maximum karmic opportunity.

In this lifetime, your soul will be presented with many challenges that are actually opportunities for you to clear your karma and grow your soul. When you look at challenges as growth opportunities, you can welcome obstacles that might otherwise discourage you and use them as literal gateways to your personal enlightenment. Here are some examples:

Addiction. You may abuse drugs (legal and/or illegal) or alcohol, overwork, overexercise or use food or other forms of distraction as a way to avoid the truth of who you really are.

Emotional Starvation. If you are suffering from the karma of emotional starvation, you don't know how to be kind and compassionate to yourself or nurture your own emotions.

Codependency. You have interwoven your personal energy with other people's energy and karma, often to the point of taking on their pain, suffering and even karma.

Deep-Seated Negative Experiences. You may have experienced trauma in this or another lifetime that has led you to experience posttraumatic stress disorder (PTSD), anxiety and/or depression.

Genetic Code Dysfunction. You may have inherited energies programming you for sickness, struggle and poverty.

Heart Scars. You may have been wounded so deeply at the heart level that the scars go all the way into your soul. The heart scars may be affecting your physical heart and energy level.

Lost Soul Fragments. In this or some other lifetime, you may have lost key aspects of yourself along the way causing you to feel incomplete and unfulfilled.

Negative Cords and Hooks. You may have allowed others to hook into your personal energy in a parasitic manner so that they are draining your personal chi and relying on your hard work and even money.

Negative Interference. No matter what you do to try to get ahead in life, something always seems to be blocking your way.

Negative Self-Image. No matter what you do to build your self-esteem, mistakes in this or some other lifetime may have convinced you that you are a "bad" person and unlovable or unworthy.

Parallel Universe Integration. You may be running multiple lifetimes at once, leading to exhaustion, misdirection and confusion.

Past Life Vows to Avoid Giving or Receiving Love. In this or any other lifetime, you may have promised not to give or receive love. You may find yourself unable to form or maintain healthy intimate relationships.

Past Life Vows to Be a Caretaker. In this or any other lifetime, you may have promised to take care of others rather than allow yourself to be taken care of.

Past Life Vows Blocking Your Creativity. In this or any other lifetime, you may have allowed your creativity to be stifled or censored.

Past Life Vows of Poverty and Chastity. In this or any other lifetime, you may have agreed to stay poor and celibate, either by joining a religious order or misunderstanding what it means to be a spiritual person.

Past Life Vows of Vengeance and Revenge. In this or any other lifetime, you may have promised to avenge a perceived wrong. Consequently, you find yourself constantly out to fight injustice.

Past Life Vows to Enslave Others or Be a Slave. In this or any other lifetime, you may have agreed to be treated as property rather than as a human being.

Past Life Vows to Deny the Presence of God Within You. You may have made a soul agreement to deny your innate spirituality.

Past Life Vows to Prevent the Personal Use of Healing Energies. You may have made a soul agreement preventing you from giving or receiving healing energy, causing you to experience constant illness.

Past Life Vows to Deny Personal Responsibility. You may have entered into a soul agreement that causes you to blame others for the life you yourself have created.

Past Life Vows to Sacrifice. You may have made a soul agreement to sacrifice your life, money or energy for the benefit of others.

Suffering. You may have entered into a soul agreement to take on world suffering, not recognizing that you also can serve by lifting your own personal vibration and thereby raising others up in your presence.

Negative Spiritual Energy. Do you have negative spiritual energies dragging down your overall vibration? A good way to think of negative spiritual energy is low frequency vibrations.

Black Magic. Either consciously or unconsciously, an individual or group of people intends for you to be harmed.

Earthbound Entities. You may be bothered by spirits who have passed out of their physical bodies but not crossed over into heaven.

Emotional Turmoil Entities. You may be unable to escape the negative emotional energy lingering in your home, office or space, e.g., because of constant fighting, domestic abuse or crime.

Fear Entities. You may be trapped by frequent anxiety,

caused by either a group of fearful people, your own expectations of failure or the energy of panic anywhere in the world.

Gloom, Doom and Disaster. You may be suffering from a low-frequency energy that often follows a war, famine, financial collapse, terrorism or other man-made calamities.

Gray Entities. Deceptive energies may try to harm you. They are often hard to spot and tend to trick you when you least expect it. They hide in the shadows and try their best to keep you from seeing what they're really doing.

Negative Spirit Attachment. A low-frequency energy may have attached itself to you. The result can be pain, suffering, anxiety or unrelenting depression and hopelessness.

Poltergeist. A ghost is a spirit responsible for upsetting disturbances.

Satanic Entities. In multiple religions, these devilish energies are known to create evil wherever they go.

How Your Soul Communicates with You

Claircognizance. Psychic knowing. You know what you need to know, often without any logical explanation.

Clairaudience. Psychic hearing. You receive information in the form of words, sounds and vibration.

Clairsentience. Psychic feeling. You pick up the energy, vibe and feelings.

Clairvoyance. Psychic vision. You receive information in visual symbols and inner pictures.

To understand more about your psychic gifts, please read my book *Unlimited Intuition Now.*

Soul Medicine That Works Best for You

Just as your body relies on good food, rest and exercise, your soul needs nurturing. These are activities you can do to feed your soul. While all of them may work for some people, certain activities may be more beneficial for your soul growth at any given point in time:

Breathwork
Prayer
Meditation
Mantras
Rest
Unscheduled Time Alone to Process
Laughter
Dancing
Time in Nature
Time with Loved Ones
Hugs
Sunlight
Fresh Air
Flowers

Companionship of a Pet
Volunteer Work
Writing
Channeling
Singing
Painting
Travel
Time Away from Home
Setting Healthy Boundaries
Companionship of Like-Minded People
Storytelling
Spiritual Retreat
Spiritual Family
Spiritual Community
Letting Go of Clutter
New Environment
New Challenges
Forgiveness
Saying I'm Sorry and Meaning It
Giving Yourself Permission to Say No
Dropping Your Masks
Giving Yourself Permission to Be Your True Self
Deep Inner Listening
Letting Go and Allowing God to Guide You

Perhaps you can think of other ways your own soul needs to be fed. Listen within and allow yourself to be guided!

Chapter 9:
Your Soul Purpose

"The basic law underlying all occult healing, may be stated to be as follows: Law I: All disease is the result of inhibited soul life . . . . The art of the healer consists in releasing the soul, so that its life can flow through the aggregate of organisms which constitute any particular form. It is interesting to note that the attempt of the scientist to release the energy of the atom, is of the same general nature as the work of the esotericist when he endeavors to release the energy of the soul. In this release the nature of the true art of healing is hidden."

- *Alice Bailey*

One of the most common questions people ask me during a medical intuitive reading is, "What is my soul purpose?"

Your soul purpose is the primary reason you were born in this lifetime.

It's why you ended up in your body with those parents.

It's why you endured the childhood you did.

It's why you've had each and every obstacle that God put in front of you.

It's why you're missing what you're missing and why you've been blessed with the gifts you do possess.

Your soul purpose is what makes your heart sing.

When you follow your soul purpose, you feel energized, uplifted, excited, on fire with joy.

Recently I was out of town, but someone needed a medical intuitive reading by a certain deadline. So, I woke up at 3:00 a.m., and conducted the reading with complete joy in my heart and awe for the soul I was exploring.

When I finished, I simply went back to sleep. Of course, I would rather do my work at 8:00 a.m., after a healthy breakfast, but here's the point:

Following your soul purpose gives you energy.

You can follow your soul purpose even when you're tired, hungry, lonely, not your best self, not dressed in your finest or otherwise indisposed. Doing what you are here to do will light up your life on every level.

Before showing up at a writing retreat recently, I had suffered a series of minor disasters:

-- Both of my websites crashed.
-- Some idiot smashed into my mailbox.
-- My accountant made a series of errors.

In each case, I had to drop everything and deal. So, when I showed up for the retreat, I wasn't sure how I would actually be able to write.

But after writing nonstop for three days, you would have thought I had just been to the spa for a week. I went back home with more energy than when I arrived.

Here's what your soul purpose IS NOT:

Your soul purpose is not your job. Think about it. Let's say you're a fireman. Is your soul purpose to put out fires? Possibly, but probably not.

Perhaps your soul purpose is to save other people's lives.

Perhaps your soul purpose is to comfort those in distress.

Perhaps your soul purpose is to protect people too defenseless to defend themselves.

Your soul purpose is not about earning money.
Although we all need to earn a living, your soul purpose has literally nothing to do with adding to your wealth or supporting your family.

You can sometimes work toward your soul purpose while earning your way, but you'd be able to pursue your soul purpose even if no one gave you a dime.

Your soul purpose isn't about you. Yes, your soul purpose is your purpose, so it is about you in that you do it, but it is bigger than you.

It's not "me" thinking.

It's not even "we" thinking.

It's all thinking.

Your soul purpose serves the higher good. It allows you to uplift yourself along with the rest of the planet.

Here are a few examples of soul purposes:

Being a good mother, father, brother, sister, uncle, aunt or friend
Creating
Leading
Inspiring
Uplifting
Enlightening
Exploring
Discovering
Supporting
Enhancing
Providing
Protecting
Growing
Learning
Healing
Overcoming
Teaching
Demonstrating

As you can see, your soul purpose is something you DO. And yet most often you will find yourself DOING your purpose simply by being YOU -- being who you are meant to be in this lifetime and the very best version of yourself.

I remember years ago waking up in the middle of the night. Thinking I might be stressed because I couldn't sleep, I went downstairs to my computer to hook myself up to a device that measured my stress level.

Instead of being stressed, I discovered I was in 100 percent entrainment -- not only perfectly balanced but in a state of complete inner peace.

At the time, I recall asking why I had been blessed with my home. It sits on a corner lot on a busy Atlanta street. People come off the interstate, drive two blocks and enter the heart of my neighborhood.

When I bought the home, it was priced significantly lower than any other house for sale in the neighborhood. In fact, I would not have been able to afford any other area house at the time or ever since.

I felt like I had won the lottery by snagging that house. Not only do I love the house, I raise an organic garden there, grow my orchids and have been able to work from my home studio for the past two decades without having to fight Atlanta traffic.

In that state of high entrainment, when I asked for guidance on why I had been blessed with my home, I was told to uplift the vibration of everyone driving past.

I had been afraid that my purpose for being blessed with the house might be something difficult, something hard for me to accomplish. But, all I had to do was live there.

Feeling thankful for my home and blessed with fresh understanding, I went upstairs to my bedroom and went right back to sleep.

Your soul purpose is like that.

You can pursue and achieve your soul purpose easily, enjoyably, just by being you!

Chapter 10:
What Does Your Soul Long to Do?

"Nothing is impossible for pure love."
- *Mahatma Gandhi*

Since I am a medical intuitive healer, people often ask me what their soul is here to do.

Your soul purpose is not the same thing as your job.

You may be able to express your soul purpose through your work. When you're in the right profession, you may feel deeply fulfilled, but what your soul longs to do will reward you more deeply than any paycheck ever can.

As you come to a closer, clearer understanding of your soul purpose, you'll experience a greater connection to all that is.

This feeling of oneness is deeply fulfilling.

This feeling of connectedness often overrides the anguish of depression, anxiety, loneliness, listlessness and diseases that previously plagued you.

Your purpose gives you the strength to carry on, the insight to understand why certain things have happened the way they did, and the tenacity to keep moving forward.

As a medical intuitive healer, I simply listen:

-- I listen to your body.

-- I listen to your energy.

-- I listen to your emotions.

-- I listen to your mind, your thoughts and beliefs, including the stories you've been telling about what you think is and is not true about yourself.

-- And, most of all, I listen to your soul because it guides your entire life experience.

I love listening to people from around the world and from all walks of life. In the past year I've listened to rock stars, Navy SEALs, CEOs, mothers, daughters, lawyers, doctors, yoga teachers, clothing designers, artists, teenagers, dogs and people so distraught they were ready to end it all right then and there.

As I listen at the soul level, here are a few observations:

1. What your soul is pursuing is bigger than you. If you are limiting yourself to "I thinking" or "me thinking," you aren't truly listening to your soul. You'd be stuck in your ego, the source of all disconnection, misery, worry, anxiety and depression.

2. Your soul longs for you to take action. If you are

feeling stuck or stagnant, treading water, or thinking you're going nowhere, you have lost touch with what your soul wants you to do.

3. As you connect to oneness by taking the right action, you resonate with true joy. If you feel disconnected from the natural bliss inherent in your soul, you have lost touch with what you're really all about.

4. The challenges you've faced in life are often directly related to your soul purpose.

   For example, if your soul purpose is healing, you may have experienced a tremendous amount of illness. If your soul purpose is forgiveness, you may have been deeply wronged. When your soul purpose is to lead, you may have faced countless challenges to your inner strength and had others question your values, opinions or reasoning. The gift of those obstacles is to ground you more firmly in what you are here to do.

As I listen at the soul level, this is what I hear souls telling me they long to do:

Create. If your soul longing is to create, you may find yourself yearning to build, paint, write, design, or establish. Although creativity is typically thought of as being the province of artists, some of the most creative people I've ever met have been entrepreneurs. They dream of establishing something that can be left behind, that makes a difference, that inspires others to see, feel or hear something from an entirely different perspective.

Express. When your soul longs to express, you hanker to release thoughts, feelings, insights, and imaginings from deep inside you so that others may benefit. The communication could take written form but may also include public speaking and musical or dance performances. Releasing your deeply held energy and emotions transforms not only your life but the lives of others.

Transcend. Your soul never intends to stand still. If your soul purpose is to transcend, you may discover yourself with tremendous personal challenges -- anxiety, depression, addiction, abuse, unthinkable poverty and many other seemingly insurmountable obstacles. You show the way for those who think they're too weak or their challenges too daunting. You demonstrate what it means to live in the present by letting go of the past.

Forgive. Although the spiritual texts encourage us to forgive ("God, forgive them for they know not what they do," or "forgive us our trespasses as we forgive those who have trespassed against us"), we must discover for ourselves the exact best methods to release the resentment, bitterness and judgment that keep our energy stuck in the past. If your soul purpose is forgiveness, you may experience many seemingly atrocious personal affronts that challenge your concepts of what is and is not forgivable.

Give. Although there is always a balance in life between giving and receiving, the first step is to open your heart and give all the way from the level of your soul. Once you comprehend that whatever you give is in fact what you also receive, you'll discover that the more you give, the more blessings become miraculously available to you. You demonstrate faith in the abundance of life by fearlessly sharing all you possess. The gifts may include not only money but also your knowledge, time and wisdom.

Grow. When your soul longs to grow, you constantly seek out new sources of spiritual nourishment so that you can expand in many directions. Learning and growing tend to go together. Your mind prepares the way as your soul grows. You naturally gravitate toward other learners and growers who can keep up with your accelerated soul path.

Heal. When your soul longs to heal, you naturally want to restore a sense of inner peace, wholeness and well-being to everyone everywhere. You may begin by healing yourself or discovering the inner alchemy of the healing arts, be it traditional medicine, Ayurveda, energy healing, food healing or all manner of natural healing.

Connect. When your soul longs to connect, you perceive the common humanity in people everywhere. Your connections may be physical, energetic, emotional, mental or spiritual. As you form invisible cord connections with others, you leave behind any illusions of separation or loneliness and feel at one with the family of man.

Explore. Whether you become a psychonaut (traversing your inner landscape) or yearn to experience the seven continents, rivers, mountains, lakes, streams, oceans, above and below, your soul delights in all of creation. You uplift others by your appreciation for the beauty and wonder of the planet and life itself.

Lead. You may find yourself suddenly out front. You may have been born with an alpha personality or discover your passion for a cause so important that you wind up steering the destiny of millions. Your inner alignment with deeper values inspires others to follow.

Love. When your life purpose is to love, you may find yourself in the humblest of circumstances expressing your appreciation, reverence and adoration for the people, places, animals and the planet's other inhabitants as well as the glory of the universe itself. You intuitively understand how much love other people put into their own contributions. You value what leads others to experience unconditional love.

Become. When your soul purpose is to become, your life is all about personal evolution. You may be born into a certain set of circumstances that are so uncomfortable, so personally detestable to you and so untenable that you find yourself forced to develop and evolve. Others may think you've undergone a tremendous transformation by deepening your wisdom, building financial assets from apparently nothing or learning to express your own highest potential.

Be. If your soul purpose is being, you may find yourself expressing the inner peace that comes from being at one with all that is. You fully accept your life circumstances, other people and the way life is without needing to fix, correct, control or edit the perfection inherent in the process.

Fulfill. If your soul purpose is fulfillment, you may identify the needs around you and find unique ways to make sure they get met. You feed the hungry, plant a tree, hug children, make friends with the homeless and teach those who are afraid how to find peace within themselves.

Share. If your soul purpose is to share, you may recognize there is no such thing as a vacuum in the universe. You may understand the truth that all material possessions are yours to play with for only a few cycles around the sun. You transcend the illusion of scarcity and contribute to the lives of others whether you share your money, wisdom, time or personal energy. You realize that all you give is quickly replaced as the well of abundance never runs dry.

Worship. When your soul purpose is to worship, you see and understand the contribution of prayer, meditation, ritual and silence. You give thanks whenever possible. You empower others to see the visible proof of God in action. You inspire faith in the process of life and a deeper understanding of the mysterious force of universal love that guides the divine unfoldment of our lives.

Nurture. When your soul purpose is to nurture, you may find yourself tending plants, hugging babies or providing comfort for those who seem to have lost their way. The universe responds to your kindness by flourishing in your very presence. You recognize that your life is about something greater than yourself, and you're happy to support the growth process for others.

As you read over these soul purposes, you may find yourself relating to many but resonating with one or two. Give yourself permission to meditate. Pray for guidance so that your own soul purpose can be revealed.

As your soul purpose becomes self-evident, the life path you have taken so far may make more sense. The way forward may become clearer.

The ego stories you have been telling yourself about why your life has seemed so difficult may now need to be rewritten.

Miracles occur as your soul purpose becomes clear in your inner vision.

Your soul leads the way in every moment of your every day. Take the time to understand what you are here to do, and discover your deeper connection to all that is.

Chapter 11:
Determined to Be Born

"Lose yourself completely. Return to the root of the root of your own soul."

- *Rumi*

Let me tell you a story. It's about you and how you may or may not have come to be born.

If I offend anybody, I apologize. If you think I'm wrong, I also apologize. I'm telling you this story based on my current understanding.

First of all, it's a privilege to be born. It's a privilege to have a body. It's a true honor to be here now in this lifetime.

If people understood how hard their soul tried to be born, there would be many fewer suicides because they would come to accept how purposeful their soul has been every moment of every day.

So, here's my story.

Your current life began at the moment of conception, when your father's sperm fertilized your mother's egg.

Through no fault of the mother, however, a pregnancy often fails to work out.

You may have tried multiple times to get born. I like to joke that maybe your first choice was that well-adjusted couple with the swimming pool over in Beverly Hills.

You could have been born into plenty of money and gotten your own car when you were 16. Shucks -- that didn't work out for you?

You try again.

And again.

And again.

For you to have tried multiple times to be born means you are a very strong soul who had a very important purpose for being here.

You wanted a Learjet, but you showed up in a donkey cart. Either way, you got here.

In my own case, my birth parents were my eighth try. Even as a little girl, before I consciously knew anything.

I remember thinking, "Who are these people?" I always related to the story of Cinderella, raised by women other than her true family.

The experience of trying to get born, and perhaps failing multiple times, affects at least one of your organs and sets you up for a predominant emotion throughout your lifetime.

For instance, your toil to be born may have affected your liver, causing you to feel constantly angry and frustrated.

Or it may have bothered your kidneys, causing you to have trouble with trust -- not trusting life, your process, or yourself.

If you realize your birth parents were just here to give you a body, it may be a whole lot easier to let go of the expectations you've been harboring.

Recognize your own needs. Find people who can be your spiritual family -- who understand and support you in all the ways you need. Then you can let go and recognize there is actually nothing to forgive.

There's nothing to fix with your birth parents, your childhood or what happened to you before you turned 18 and matured into adulthood.

Just unconditional acceptance.

Just gratitude.

Get on with what you're here to do. Free yourself with the knowledge you have more important things to do than hang on to the past.

Book II
Massive Characters Seared with Scars

"Out of suffering have emerged the strongest souls; the most massive characters are seared with scars."

- Khalil Gibran

Chapter 1:
The Healer Who Processed Planetary Grief

"It is both a blessing and a curse to feel everything so very deeply."

- *David Jones*

Lincoln (not his real name) had been a successful real estate investor whose life nearly came to a complete halt after he got sick from surfing. He traveled the world and spent hundreds of thousands of dollars trying to resolve the illness, which almost killed him.

Then, Lincoln met a medical intuitive healer who diagnosed him in five minutes: It was red tide poisoning, a phenomenon caused by algal blooms, which are large concentrations of aquatic microorganisms.

After his health was restored, Lincoln dedicated himself to natural healing. He established a center where people from around the world could come to experience plant medicines.

When Lincoln and I had our first medical intuitive reading, I explained he had been processing grief on behalf of the entire planet.

"You are among the top 2 percent of the most sensitive people in the world," I observed. "You are deeply sensitive to what is happening. You are grieving the state of humanity.

"You literally feel grief about what is happening to the environment and to animals.

"On the one hand, the grief motivates you, but you want to be able to stay motivated without having to process it yourself."

Although Lincoln had become incredibly healthy again, the planetary grief he had been processing continued to affect his lungs. "In some weird way, you are doing it as a form of service," I explained. "You have to realize that you can serve even better if you do not take on the grief."

Swimming in the ocean three or four times a week would help William to clear his energy field, I suggested, as would calling on the Dolphin power animal. (Power animals are spiritual beings who work in other dimensions to support our soul purpose.)

I asked Lincoln to tune in to his power animal's message, and Dolphin said, "You don't have to do this all by yourself!"

I also recommended a flower essence made from orchids that empowers you to heal from the soul's darkest experiences.

Lincoln was so sensitive, I explained, that even if he couldn't immediately acquire the remedy, he could meditate on a photograph of the orchid the essence was made from and receive the same benefits.

"You almost do better with energy medicine than you do with actual substances," I said.

"You have a high level of intelligence about energy medicine. When you realize a vibration that you personally need, you are able to tune into that."

William could overdose on actual supplements very quickly because all he needed was the vibration. "That may have been why you had trouble with doctors and medications. Even with natural supplements, you can get too much.

"You have the capacity of tuning into people and giving them the precise vibrational frequency they need to bring themselves into balance.

"You just intuitively know the right frequency."

"If someone went to a homeopath, the homeopath would prescribe the frequency to come up with the remedy. For you, just by meeting people, you know the frequency they need."

Lincoln has the same psychic gift I do: claircognizance, the ability to know the unknown.

Although Lincoln had used his gift to make millions in business, his exquisite sensitivity was even better suited to his true soul calling as a healer.

The red tide illness that nearly killed him had actually been a soul-level adjustment so that he could move forward with his soul longing to uplift the vibration of the entire planet.

Chapter 2:
My Past Life as an Ayurvedic Practitioner

"You must form the habit of living in the fourth dimension, 'The World of the Wondrous.' It is the world where you do not judge by appearances."

- Florence Scovel Shinn

About a year ago, I asked a friend to hypnotize me. Although past life regression isn't the modality I typically turn to for insight, given the level of skill I have as a medical intuitive healer, I figured I must have done similar work in multiple past lifetimes and wanted to know more.

I was not disappointed.

As I journey into one lifetime in my mind's eye, I look down at my feet and discover myself to be a thin, barefoot, dark brown man wearing a silvery grey turban and a loin cloth. I live in the jungles of India.

My spiritual guides tell me the year is 1881.

I'm a holy man, about 35 years old at the time.

I've got a small brass bowl for rice, and people come to me one by one. I put my hands on them and pray with and for them.

At the same time, I'm looking at them in the eyes, straight into the eyes, all the way down to their soul. Just by looking,

I can see everything.

After I look into their eyes, I pray for them again.

Two scribes are sitting with me. I mumble some words, and they write everything down.

I tell the scribes which herbs will make each person better. I’m not handing out the herbs myself, but I give the scribes a verbal list of what each individual needs. The scribes then give each person a piece of paper.

When we’re done, everyone brings their hands together in a gesture of Namaste, acknowledging the divinity in one another.

At the end of the day, the scribes and I pray and meditate together for about two or three hours.

I sleep on a simple pallet. It doesn't look very comfortable, but I have a big connection to the moon and make sure I can see it every night.

It's as if the moon helps me to maintain my own internal circadian rhythm.

As I move forward in the lifetime, war erupts, and a lot of people are dying or injured. In fact, so many people are injured that I can't personally heal everyone. All I can do is pray and meditate.

I'm calling on the vibrations of peace to bring more tranquility into the land. It's funny because somehow or another, it's like I'm calling on the earth's energy to shift what has just happened.

Thousands of people have been injured or are dying, and there are too many of them. So I just call on the vibration -- a deep calmness -- to restore peace.

I'm instructing two young scribes to pray with me because the injuries and the affliction are so great that our herbs won't help.

When it's time for me to die, I am out walking and get bitten by a long, green snake. Although I know how to heal myself from the snakebite, it's OK because I feel my work has been done.

I'm ready to go.

Chapter 3:
My Past Life as an Indian Medicine Woman

"To be in time is to sleep; to be awake is to be in eternity."
- *Osho*

A second hypnosis regresses me to another lifetime.

As I awake, I find myself living in a teepee somewhere along a river in the plains. I am about 56 years old with long black hair.

My teepee is full of musical instruments including rattles, drums and a horn.

As a medicine woman, I use the musical instruments in ceremonies to mark changes in the seasons and important events in the life of the community.

In this lifetime, I'm also the person who prays with everyone.

I worship to numerous gods and pray for rain and for the men who are hunting. I'm praying for everyone in the village, the whole community, the whole tribe.

As I move forward into that lifetime, I see myself leading some kind of ceremony, and we're passing around a pipe full of herbs.

It isn't safe in the village anymore. We realize we must move and are praying for guidance on where to go next.

The ceremony continues for two or three days.

I'm the person who's supposed to capture and share the vision with the whole community. I'm seeing that we need to move into the mountains. We've been down in a valley for a while, and now we need to head to the hills.

When I get the vision, I tell the village elders. Then the whole tribe packs up and hits the trail for about two and a half weeks. Everyone is carrying things. Even the small children are helping.

When it's time for me to die, I go off into the mountains -- not eating or drinking, just waiting.

I am at peace and ready to go.

I ask for peace to be brought upon my tribe. I want everyone who's left behind to be safe and healthy.

As I pass away, my spirit rises up into the sky like a hawk. Up in the clouds, I look down at the mountains and then fly over my village to make sure everyone's safe and OK.

People are crying. My son is in tears. At the same time, he realizes I went away because I was ready to go.

My son looks up into the sky and sees a hawk. He forms a connection with me as the hawk, and I let him know that for the rest of his life, I will be there with him. Whenever he needs me, he can just look up to the sky and find the hawk.

Chapter 4:
The Psychic Navy SEAL

"If knocked down I will get back up, every time. I will draw on every remaining ounce of strength to protect my teammates and to accomplish our mission. I am never out of the fight."

- Marcus Luttrell

Jax (not his real name) had been a member of the SEALS, the U.S. Navy's elite special ops branch, before working for the Central Intelligence Agency (CIA) for 10 years.

Jax left the CIA because he didn't like the people. "They are a bunch of backstabbing snakes," he told me with disgust.

Although Jax had been working as a bodyguard since leaving the government, he had not found his calling in civilian life. A friend referred him to me for a medical intuitive reading so I could help him see the kind of work that he would be a natural fit for.

As I performed the reading, I could see Jax's energy field had been shattered by the numerous traumas he had experienced in military life. If you could see what I saw, it would resemble a shattered window after someone had thrown a bunch of rocks at it.

The breaks in Jax's energetic field had made him exquisitely sensitive to all kinds of energy -- scanners at the airport, electromagnetic frequencies such as cell phones, other people's emotions. But they hadn't changed the core of his soul.

Although Jax hadn't thought of himself as intuitive, I explained his primary psychic gift is claircognizance or psychic knowing.

Most people think of psychics as women in purple robes telling fortunes to the lovelorn, not truly understanding just how valuable and lifesaving the skill can be.

Claircognizance is the highest psychic gift.

When you receive information in this way, you know whatever you need to know in less than 30 seconds. It's not only the fastest psychic gift, but it gives you advance information, often with no forewarning or any supporting evidence.

"If someone saw you, they might think you are just a big lug, but in fact you are very highly intelligent," I explained to Jax. "What comes across to people is your physical presence, so they may miss your IQ.

"In fact, you have a genius IQ.

"You are a leader, a teacher and a tracker.

"You have a very large ethical mindset, so well-established

you can decide right from wrong in split seconds."

Jax's ethical mindset and ability to discern right from wrong had left him with a deep sense of rage as he could see right through most people. His ability to see the games people were playing also had left him with a profound level of distrust.

It was a big deal for Jax to trust me enough to have a medical intuitive reading. He had been referred by one of his best friends, a guy Jax considered part of his team. Their cadre of friends was so close and had been through so much together they even had a secret name for their brotherhood.

"You have all this rage inside you -- bigger than your heart chakra," I explained to Jax. "It's taking over your chest area. You have to learn how to channel it. You haven't figured it out yet.

"Up until now you haven't had a good method for releasing your rage. The previous method was being at war.

"You also used your anger to get through the SEAL training.

"Energy can neither be created nor destroyed. You have to channel it."

Being high in claircognizance -- knowing the unseen -- and

the ability to read people like a book made Jax very good at tracking, I explained. "You would be very good at finding people who don't want to be found."

I told Jax his power animal is Wolf, which gives him the ability to be the natural leader of the pack.

"I see you running teams of guys who are finding people. These are shady characters who exist in the grey area. They are not legal, but maybe not illegal, and also transnational, all over the world.

"Corporations want to catch these people who are breaking into businesses, especially in China and Hong Kong.

"Do this as your own business.

"I see no women in this company. You are a true protector, and a lot of this isn't safe.

"Your customers are companies who want to find people -- bad people who are interfering with their businesses. They want you to find these people so they will stop interfering with their businesses.

"Study the wolf to help you see what you're supposed to be creating and how you're supposed to be working."

Some people don't do well in a 9-to-5 office situation. Jax was certainly one of them!

His soul purpose was leadership.

Sitting on the sidelines and not having a pack to lead, Jax felt deeply ill at ease.

Coming into alignment with his soul purpose would ignite the passion and make Jax feel fully alive again.

Chapter 5:
You Survive Everything Until You Don't

"Wake up to the unchanging in you."
- *Jaggi Vasudev, Sadhguru*

What does it mean to know yourself as a soul?

At certain points in your life, you may identify yourself as something you actually aren't:

When you identify yourself as your body, you are overly identified with yourself as a human animal. Certainly, you have a physical body. The aches and pains, the need to fill up or empty out, the hormonal drives -- all are valid and at times all-encompassing aspects of being alive in this lifetime. But you are not your body.

.

When you identify yourself as your energy, you may be obsessed with being tired all the time or feeling overly excited. The energy coursing through you may feel like something to refill or use somehow. Your energy is as unique to you as your thumbprint -- very different than anyone else's -- but that still isn't who you actually are.

When you identify yourself as your emotions, you may be preoccupied with shame, guilt, apathy, grief, fear, desire, anger, pride, anxiety, depression or any other feelings. Certainly, your emotions can be excellent guides to show what serves you or detracts from the joy of being fully alive in this lifetime. But if you observe your emotions, they may come and go like the weather. It may rain, but it doesn't rain all the time. You may feel sad, but you probably don't feel that way every moment of every day.

When you identify yourself as your mind, you may be overly identified with the ego persona you have developed over time. You may see yourself as a "good" person or a "bad" person. You may be overly identified with the roles you play -- e.g., holding down a job or being a mother/father/brother/sister/uncle/aunt with your victim, saboteur, inner child, prostitute or any other persona you have become accustomed to playing. The roles are part of your facade. During the course of a day, you may switch from role to role as often as you change clothes. You aren't your ego, and you certainly aren't your carefully crafted self-image.

When you wake up to the unchanging you, you recognize that through it all -- your birth, childhood, adolescence, adulthood and old age -- there's a part of you that actually feels the same. Young people are often surprised to hear that older adults feel the same on the inside as they did when they were 22.

When you recognize yourself as soul, you come to accept that you have a purpose you and you alone can fulfill in this lifetime. The recognition of who you are and the purpose you are to fulfill gives a certain urgency to your life. You want to get on with it! You recognize the preciousness of life itself. You value every moment, treasuring the sunrises and sunsets. In a very humble way, you recognize that you are important, your presence matters, and who you are changes everything.

When you accept your eternal self, you realize that every person you meet in your lifetime has a purpose for being here. Even if your ego labels the other characters as "bad" or "good" or as people you like or dislike, you come to recognize they are here for your highest good. They may be your teachers. They may be people you have the opportunity to uplift. They may be people with whom you have important soul contracts to fulfill. You recognize the meaning of the word "Namaste." Your divine self recognizes the divinity in all others.

When you honor the divinity in yourself, you come to see yourself and all others as being on a hero's journey. Some chapters in your life may be times to rest, to stabilize, to consolidate. But most of the time you will find yourself battling dragons, riding the waves of rough seas, venturing from the known into the unknown, meeting others who help you on your way, and experiencing little deaths and little rebirths that pave the way for major transformation.

When you recognize the eternal part of you, you know you survived everything that ever happened to you -- falling off your bike, having your heart broken again and again, losing your job, going through a divorce, cracking your ribs, going in and out of hospitals, suffering the death of loved ones and encountering any of a thousand other human tragedies. This recognition of the survivor in you --

the one who makes it through everything until you don't -- gives you tremendous courage to give your whole spirit to life.

The journey to discovering who you actually are -- the eternal hero with a spiritual purpose -- is part of what fascinates me whenever I do a soul reading.

Have you woken up to who you are?

Have you embraced your life purpose?

Have you let go of the ego identification with your body, energy, emotions, and mental pictures of yourself?

Do you really know yourself as soul?

Chapter 6:
Prayer for My Reader

Heavenly Father,

I say a special prayer now for my dear reader, this precious reader.

Please help this reader to come to know himself or herself as soul.

Please bless this reader with the knowledge that he or she is in fact a soul living in this body in this lifetime.

Please empower this reader to embrace the strength, wisdom, tenacity, unconditional love and experience of their timeless soul.

Please bless them with a deep reverence for their life itself, awakening them to their soul purpose so that they treasure every moment of every precious day, realizing their very presence makes a difference.

Thank you for blessing this dear reader with this insight.

I ask that this be done in the name of Jesus Christ.

Thank you God, thank you God, thank you God.

Amen.

Chapter 7:
How Your Soul Communicates with You

"The soul, or life within us, by no means agrees with the life outside us. If one has the courage to ask her what she thinks, she is always saying the very opposite to what other people say."

- *Virginia Woolf*

Many people think psychic gifts are the province of someone else -- certainly not you. It is my belief and experience, however, that your soul is always trying to communicate with you.

You are not your body.

You are not your ego.

You are your soul.

As you learn to listen to your soul, you can receive guidance at the soul level. This inner direction can serve you in every aspect of your life, leading you to all that's for your highest good.

The trick is to learn how your soul communicates with you.

Here are four simple ways your soul may communicate:

Claircognizance. You just know stuff. You know what

you need to know when you know it. You may not know how you know, you just do.

When your soul communicates with you through this gift, information comes in very fast. If it takes you longer than 30 seconds to get an answer, it's not your soul speaking. It's your ego.

Clairaudience. You may hear a voice or voices without being certifiably crazy. You also may hear sounds or sense vibrations. This gift is often confused with your own thoughts.

When your soul communicates with you through this gift, you also receive swift answers. And if it takes longer than 30 seconds, you're allowing your ego to slip in with its own opinions.

Clairsentience. You pick up the vibes, the feelings, the energy. This gift often confuses how other people feel with the way you actually feel.

When your soul communicates with you through this gift, you need to take time to process the energy and information you receive.

Allow yourself to feel how you feel, both your emotions and your body sensations. Also allow yourself plenty of time to sense the environment around you. This is one of the slowest gifts, but it feels very real.

Clairvision. You may see auras or angels or observe inner visions in your dreams. You may receive images as symbols. When you receive a vision, you still must interpret what it means.

When your soul communicates through clairvision, give yourself permission to manifest into physical reality the picture your soul shows you in your inner vision.

To learn more about your gifts in greater detail, read or listen to the audiobook version of my book *Unlimited Intuition Now*.

Chapter 8:
What Are Soul Wounds?

"You pierce my soul. I am half agony, half hope . . . . I have loved none but you."

- Jane Austen

Soul wounds are insults you may have experienced in this or another lifetime that have gone so deep they affect you to the level of your soul.

Let me tell you a very unusual story.

Years ago, a gentleman in a business suit brought his young daughter to work with me for help resolving learning difficulties.

The daughter was so young I sat on the floor with her. To any outside observer, what I was doing would have looked like she and I were just playing.

As a medical intuitive healer, I always adapt what I'm doing so that the person I'm working with feels most at ease.

I didn't hear from the gentleman or his little girl for a few weeks, but when I did, he called and asked me a question.

"The school wants to know what it is that you do exactly?"

The little girl had made such a profound shift that the

gentleman, an international businessman I will call Eric, became my client.

Eric had a number of challenges he wanted to address. One was chronic back pain.

As I started to do healing work, what Eric needed weren't my usual recommendations for yoga stretches or chiropractic work -- as helpful as those approaches may have been. In his case, he needed to clear soul wounds.

I saw clairvoyantly that in another lifetime Eric had been gored in the upper back by a wild beast -- I'm not sure which animal, but it had a tusk.

In yet another lifetime, Eric had experienced physical torture. The funny part was that he admitted using torture-related words in his everyday speech, e.g., "I'm going to put you on the rack!"

We cleared the soul wounds, and Eric's back pain dramatically shifted. His physical body reflected what his soul had experienced over previous lifetimes.

While your physical body may indeed reflect what has happened to you in this and other lifetimes, so does your emotional body.

Let's relate those soul wounds to emotions associated with your acupuncture system:

Central Meridian. When you suffer soul wounds affecting the central meridian -- your primary yin meridian -- you may feel that no matter what you do or how hard you try, you always feel like a failure.

Governing Meridian. When you suffer soul wounds affecting the governing meridian -- your primary yang meridian -- you may feel that no matter what you do, you don't feel grounded to the earth or supported in your life's journey.

Heart Meridian. When you suffer soul wounds affecting the heart meridian, you may feel that no matter what you do, you don't know who you are or how to be happy.

Small Intestine Meridian. When you suffer soul wounds affecting the small intestine meridian, you may notice yourself making the same mistakes over and over again. You have trouble learning from your life's experiences.

Triple Warmer Meridian. When you suffer soul wounds affecting the triple warmer meridian, you may feel that no matter what you do, you aren't in harmony with the world around you.

Heart Protector Meridian. When you suffer soul wounds affecting the heart protector meridian, you may feel that no matter how hard you try, you don't feel connected to who you really are or the world around you. You constantly feel like you don't fit in.

Spleen Meridian. When you suffer soul wounds affecting the spleen meridian, you feel constantly anxious and worried about the future.

Stomach Meridian. When you suffer soul wounds affecting the stomach meridian, no matter how much you achieve, you never feel content or fulfilled.

Large Intestine Meridian. When you suffer soul wounds affecting the large intestine meridian, you literally can't let go of past hurts and regrets. You tend to stay stuck in depression.

Lung Meridian. When you suffer soul wounds affecting the lung meridian, no matter how awesome you are, you suffer from grief and low self-esteem.

Kidney Meridian. When you suffer soul wounds affecting the kidney meridian, no matter how brave you try to be, you can't move past fear.

Bladder Meridian. When you suffer soul wounds affecting the bladder meridian, you try to control yourself, your life and everyone around you. As this approach is pretty much impossible to accomplish, you tend to feel out of control most of the time.

Liver Meridian. When you suffer soul wounds affecting the liver meridian, you have trouble being kind to yourself and stay stuck in anger and frustration. You tend to block your own creativity.

Gallbladder Meridian. When you suffer soul wounds affecting the gallbladder meridian, you tend to have trouble making the right choices for yourself and the entire universe.

As you read over the list you may notice you're currently suffering from more than one soul wound.

It isn't uncommon for me to find a person with soul wounds in each and every meridian.

Chapter 9:
How to Clear Soul Wounds

"Do not be afraid of your difficulties. Do not wish you could be in other circumstances than you are. For when you have made the best of an adversity, it becomes the stepping stone to a splendid opportunity."

- Helena Petrovna Blavatsky

Just as your body can heal, so can your soul. Here's how to clear soul wounds:

Step One. Identify the meridian or multiple meridians where you are carrying soul wounds.

Step Two. Reflect. How have the soul wounds shown up in your life? Have you been punishing yourself, protecting yourself or shutting yourself off from life in a vain attempt to avoid being hurt again?

Step Three. Formulate an affirmation. I will be giving you an affirmation for each meridian, but you may want to come up with your own better way of expressing what you mean.

Central Meridian
I am a success.
I feel successful.

Governing Meridian
I ground my energy to the earth.
I feel supported now in every aspect of my life.

Heart Meridian
I know who I am.
I love my life.
I radiate happiness wherever I go.

Small Intestine Meridian
I learn from all my past experiences.
I take in what I need from life.

Triple Warmer Meridian
I am in harmony with my true self.
I am in tune with the highest and best vibrations of the universe.

Heart Protector Meridian
I am connected to my mind, body and soul.
I fit in.
I belong to a meaningful spiritual community.

Spleen Meridian
I walk by faith.
I relax and allow the process of my life to unfold.

Stomach Meridian
I feel deeply fulfilled.
I am enough, I have enough, I do enough.

Large Intestine Meridian
I let go of all that no longer serves me.
I let go and let God.

Lung Meridian
I value who I truly am.
I treasure the wonder and beauty of the universe.

Kidney Meridian
I trust God.
I welcome the divine unfolding of my life.

Bladder Meridian
I am safe.
I have patience with the process of my life.

Step Four. Bring your thumb together with your little finger and ring finger. In kinesiology, this hand mode is used to access the spiritual realm.

Then tap a big circle around your ears while repeating your affirmation.

Meanwhile, activate different parts of your brain with eye movement, looking:

UP
DOWN
RIGHT
LEFT

Then close your eyes and continue repeating the affirmation, looking:

UP
DOWN
RIGHT
LEFT

Breathe, relax and trust the process. Your soul knows how to heal itself. You only have to set your intention to do so!

Chapter 10:
Soul Medicines for Soul Wounds

"The soul should always stand ajar, ready to welcome the ecstatic experience."

- Emily Dickinson

Just as your physical body may require medication or natural healing remedies, your soul also needs medicines.

Years ago, I recall meditating with a group of Buddhist monks, who taught me a simple technique they called Medicine Buddha.

Sitting in a cross-legged position, you put your left hand upwards. You then set your intention to receive the precise frequency you need from God to heal your mind, body and spirit at this time.

All illness is slowed-down energy, and healing happens when you simply uplift the frequency. Therefore, many methods you may not have thought of as innately healing can in fact lead to profound transformation.

Here are some medicines I believe work very effectively to heal the wounded soul:

Prayer
Meditation
Breathwork

Mantras
Rest
Unscheduled Time
Laughter
Dancing
Time in Nature
Time with Loved Ones
Hugs
Sunlight
Fresh Air
Flowers
Companionship of a Pet
Volunteer Work
Writing
Singing
Painting
Travel
Time Away from Home
Setting Healthy Boundaries
Companionship of Like-Minded People
Storytelling
Spiritual Retreat
Spiritual Family
Spiritual Community
Letting Go of Clutter
New Environment
New Challenges
Forgiveness
Saying I'm Sorry and Meaning It
Giving Yourself Permission to Say No
Dropping Your Masks

Giving Yourself Permission to Be Your True Self
Letting Go and Allowing God to Heal You
Deep Inner Listening

As you read over the list, zero in on the soul medicines that speak to you at this time in your life.

What will soothe you?

What will feed you at the deepest levels?

What will uplift your soul at this time?

Give yourself permission to feed your soul, and notice how the rest of you -- your body and mind -- recovers so much more quickly.

Chapter 11:
Lou Gehrig's Disease Takes a Mother

"Only through experience of trial and suffering can soul be strengthened, ambition inspired, and success achieved."

- Helen Keller

Sarah was a petite, brilliant woman who had raised a brood of highly educated children. In fact, her kids were so smart every single one had graduated from Ivy League colleges.

A daughter who had graduated from Harvard asked me to help her mother.

By the time I went to see Sarah, her Lou Gehrig's disease -- a progressive, fatal neurological disorder -- had worsened to the point she could no longer speak.

I was the perfect person to work with Sarah because I could tune in and say, "Today you are feeling . . . "

She could nod her head and feel understood. With a traditional therapist, she could only sit and cry.

When I conducted a medical intuitive reading about the origins of Sarah's severe illness, I was surprised to discover the true causes.

For one, she had been a smoker for only one year of her relatively short life. "Let that be a lesson for all who think smoking even for a short period of time can't hurt you," I remember thinking to myself.

Second and perhaps even more important, at the soul level, Sarah had chosen Lou Gehrig's disease so that God's work could be made manifest. She was so deeply loved, so profoundly revered, that her deterioration and eventual demise had brought the entire family not only closer together but to their knees.

As high-functioning and super-achieving as they all had been, her children, grandchildren and husband had been forced to reconsider practically every aspect of their own lives after witnessing Sarah's progressive illness.

What's really important?

How much time should you actually spend at the office?

How do you handle yourself when faced with a situation that you can't actually control? Those were just some of the issues Sarah's loved ones were facing.

It was an illness that never gave up. Its relentless path wore everybody down, not just Sarah.

They had to watch as their beloved mother lost her previously magnificent capacities.

Sometimes a soul chooses a path so challenging that we draw others into deeper questions.

Why am I here?

What have I been giving?

I very much enjoyed my time with Sarah. Even though she could communicate only by scribbling a few words on a yellow legal pad she carried, she was open to understanding everything.

Sarah wanted to know all about her past lives and why she herself had become ill, often asking questions so quickly I could hardly keep up.

At times, the hurt runs so deep that nothing material -- literally nothing other than God -- can fill the void.

And that was Sarah's soul purpose for choosing Lou Gehrig's disease.

Book III
Working Out Your Salvation

"Work out your own salvation. Do not depend on others."

- Buddha

Chapter 1:
The Selfless Soul

"If the only prayer you ever say in your entire life is thank you, it will be enough."

\- *Meister Eckhart*

At a large convention years ago, a woman sitting next to me turned and said, "I don't know who you are or what you do, but I know you're supposed to help me."

Indeed.

Even though I was out of town attending a conference with thousands of other people, I agreed to work with her.

We found a small room so I could perform a medical intuitive reading and healing work.

It turned out the lady, whom I will call Hillary, was a psychotherapist.

Even though Hillary had done tremendous inner work to come to terms with the fact she had been adopted as a child, she still suffered from deep feelings of abandonment.

During the reading, I discovered the truth about her birth process was quite the opposite of what she had imagined.

On the surface, her birth mother was a loser. Unwed.

Drug-addicted. Giving up Hillary for good had caused her so much pain she fell deeper into drugs and alcohol, never truly getting over what she considered to be the biggest mistake of her life.

The little information Hillary had about her birth mother left her feeling not only abandoned but deeply ashamed of her origins.

She was worried about the kind of person who had birthed her and the possible genetic predispositions she had been carrying.

When I looked deeper into the circumstances, Hillary and her birth mother had a soul agreement. Her mother had agreed to give up her life -- quite literally -- so Hillary could be born.

Her health and self-esteem, her previous ambitions -- none of that mattered as much to the soul of the mother as passing along to Hillary the gift of life itself.

Hillary had a strong purpose for being born. Her soul had tried many times to be incarnated into a body, but none of the previous efforts had panned out.

As I explained her birth mother's true origin story, Hillary experienced a minor miracle.

A miracle is an extraordinary event manifesting divine intervention in human affairs. And the greatest miracle of all is the awareness of love's presence in your life.

Rather than seeing her birth mother as a loser, Hillary for the first time realized her mom had been her greatest benefactor.

Hillary wept at the news. Souls are actually that generous. Her mother had been that generous.

Once Hillary understood what had happened at the soul level, she realized there was nothing to forgive.

Instead of seeing her birth mother as a loser, Hillary could view the woman who gave her life as exactly what she was -- a selfless soul.

Chapter 2:
The One-Way Soul Contract

He did not say, "You will not be troubled, you will not be belabored, you will not be affected;" but he said: "You will not be overcome."

- *Mother Julian of Norwich*

Years ago, a client came to me with hepatitis (inflammation of the liver) so bad his skin looked as yellow as a legal pad. When he walked in my door on the first day, I said, "We should take a picture of you now because very shortly you will look and feel like a totally different person."

Although a lot of our work together did indeed include physical detoxification, my client (let's call him "Ray") recognized that the better part of his illness had been triggered by his anger over a failed relationship.

While Ray was drinking his smoothies and making juices from the organic parsley I gave him from my garden every week, we discussed what had led up to his liver disease.

As a gay man, Ray had been thrilled to meet the man he had hoped would become his long-term partner.

As their relationship progressed, however, Ray felt heartbroken to learn his loved one had stolen money from him. It wasn't enough that Ray had set him up in a career in the music business.

When I led a medical intuitive reading to explore the situation further, I discovered Ray and his former lover had made a soul contract together.

When I'm looking at soul contracts, I always explain there are three kinds:

> -- I may be here to help you but get nothing in return.
>
> -- You may be here to help me and expect no obvious rewards.
>
> -- Or we may have a soul contract of mutual benefit. I'm here to help you, and you're here to help me.

We expect life to be fair.

And of course, our personal definition of "fair" means I come out ahead or maybe, at the very least, equal.

As it turned out, Ray had made a soul agreement to serve his lover. At the soul level, he expected nothing in return. It wasn't supposed to look "fair" at the ego level or the financial level.

When Ray began to understand the kind of soul agreement he had made, he could let go of the bitterness and resentment that had caused his liver to inflame.

Six weeks later, during an appointment, Ray's medical doctor bet him a dinner at a five-star restaurant that he wasn't feeling well.

“Define well,” Ray replied.

“Liver enzymes below 100,” the doctor said.

The doctor lost the bet. Ray had made a radical recovery -- no drugs, no surgery, just soul-level understanding.

And the skin on his face looked radiant once again.

Ray could see his relationship for what it had in fact been -- a one-way soul contract.

Chapter 3:
Not So Fragile After All

"The smallest thing when done for the love of God is priceless."

- St. Teresa of Avila

Margaret was the middle child of an abusive father. When she was growing up, her father would get drunk and want to hit someone.

Margaret would stand between her father and her brother and sister, literally absorbing his blows to protect the others.

Her physical body reflected the abuse she had experienced. She was a large woman with a huge protective covering, a layer of fat that no diet could seem to reduce.

Margaret had gone from one therapist and healer to another, trying in vain to recover from her abusive childhood.

When I conducted a medical intuitive reading, I discovered Margaret and her father had a soul contract.

Margaret had been far too sensitive as a soul and had chosen to learn strength. And, at the soul level, her father had agreed to teach her.

At the level of her ego story, her father had been a monster, and she had been his victim.

It's so easy for us to see life that way -- as one perpetrator/victim dynamic after another. But what's really happening at the soul level?

Are the monsters we project really that evil? Are we actually victims?

When Margaret and I discussed her soul agreement, she realized her father's soul had in fact been one of her very best friends.

Margaret had never really understood why she kept choosing to stand between her crazy drunk father and her brother and sister. Yeah, she didn't want the little ones to get hurt. She didn't really want to get hurt either, but she stood up to him again and again.

Now it all made sense!

The resilience Margaret learned as a child had paid off. She had become an entrepreneur running her own business and had finally created a loving relationship through a happy marriage with her husband.

Once Margaret realized she had chosen the abuse, it was easy for her to forgive her father. She welcomed the knowledge that despite her extreme sensitivity, she had learned how to be strong.

Chapter 4:
What Is Karma?

"Accustom yourself continually to make many acts of love, for they enkindle and melt the soul."

- St. Teresa of Avila

Although many wiser sages have weighed in on the issue, please allow me to share from my perspective as a medical intuitive healer what I believe karma is all about.

In a nutshell, your karma is the energy you have created. It's the result of all your actions -- not only from this lifetime but from past lifetimes. It includes your missteps, your wise steps, your meandering, and your experiment-tation with possibility.

Karma affects you on four levels:

-- Through the thoughts in your mind.

-- Through your DNA and the energy you carry forward from your ancestors.

-- Through your soul contracts.

-- And all the way to the core of your soul.

Thoughts. You may already be aware that your thoughts create your reality. But how did your thoughts get there in the first place?

You may believe you're the one thinking the thoughts and being that they are indeed going on in your head, they certainly feel and appear to belong to you.

However, many times we pick up our thoughts from the family around us, the culture we grow up in, even in the nations where we live.

In natural healing, we call these genomes (genetic thought patterns) and miasmas (or cultural patterns).

For example, do you believe it's difficult to earn a living? If so, did you pick that thought up from your family of origin, the culture you grew up in or the country where you live?

Many thoughts you think are yours are actually *our* thoughts, belonging to and originating with a group of people larger than you.

The fact that your thoughts also belong to others doesn't make them true or false. What it does do, however, is create an energy field.

If you participate in the thoughts of your family, culture or nation state, you will then more than likely experience their karma.

That's why it's so important to examine your own thoughts, asking yourself whether they are actually true.

Even if your thoughts appear to be true at any given time, do you want them to be true for you? Maybe there is a better way of thinking that will produce results more to your liking.

DNA. Much of our karma comes through our inherited energies.

Years ago, I worked with a woman who believed that when you get to be 35, you're likely to have a hysterectomy. That had certainly been the case for her mother, aunt and sister.

Were the family members creating a thought field that led them to experience weakness in their female organs, or were they dealing with genetic abnormalities?

Many times, if you've been working hard to overcome a thought pattern, you may want to focus on your DNA.

Look at the patterns from both your mother's and your father's sides. What health issues did they pass along to you? What belief patterns do they hold?

I remember working with a client who had been sober for seven years. Unfortunately, staying clean was still a struggle.

"I have swept this floor and swept this floor and swept this floor!" she said to me with exasperation.

The thought pattern hadn’t started with her, I explained. Therefore, despite how hard she had been working, she hadn't been able to clear it completely.

She hadn't factored in the karma she had been bringing forward from her ancestors.

Soul Contracts. As we've discussed, there are three kinds of soul contracts, none of them better or worse. All are sacred.

1. You make a soul agreement to serve another soul. It’s OK with your soul that you don’t receive an apparent payoff. Souls are far more selfless than our egos!

2. Another soul is here to serve your soul. The other soul is happy to help you.

3. Or, lastly, you have a mutual agreement with another soul to help each other.

Sometimes our greatest enemies on the ego level are our very best friends on the soul level.

If you can identify what kind of soul contract you have with another person, you can complete the agreement and be done with it. That way, you don’t have to keep suffering.

You honor what you agreed to do and complete the pact.

Core of Your Soul. Sometimes the patterns you have been suffering from are so deep they go all the way to the core of your soul.

You may have been struggling with this karma for multiple lifetimes, repeating similar mistakes, and seeing the situation from multiple vantage points to work through all the layers of the issue.

Whether you've been carrying your karma in your thoughts, your DNA, your soul contracts or all the way to the core of your soul, just realize you have the ability to clear it.

If you understand that this lifetime is a field of maximum karmic opportunity, you can welcome the challenges as they arise and give yourself permission to grow at the soul level as you overcome them.

Chapter 5:
Your Karma Clearing To-Do List

"Every thought, action, decision, or feeling creates an eddy in the interlocking, inter-balancing energy fields of life. In this interconnected universe, every improvement we make in our private world improves the world at large for everyone."

- Dr. David Hawkins

Before going to the grocery store, you often may come up with a list:

Butter
Sugar
Flour
Salt
Maybe a fresh vegetable or two
Something for lunch
Something for dinner
Cookies for the dog
Kibbles for the cat
And so on.

Your karma is your unfinished spiritual business. On a soul level, it's your to-do list.

When you go to the grocery, you may have a lot of stuff to pick up on certain days and not so much on others. Similarly, some of us have more karma to clear than others.

You may know people whose lives seem to veer from one unbelievable tragedy to another. Now you know why!

And perhaps you yourself have careened from pillar to post, flung from one drama to the next, never really feeling like you've had a moment to breathe.

Maybe your soul has been a bit too ambitious and is simply trying to grow a lot in one single lifetime!

I remember once attending a workshop where the leaders began to play the sound of a mother's heartbeat.

Other people in the room started to feel warm, cozy, happy, comforted.

I literally started having a panic attack!

When I realized I had been listening to the first sounds my soul would have heard in this body in this lifetime, I understood.

I had made soul agreements to conquer so much in this lifetime. At the start of my journey, when I realized where I was and what I had signed up for, the only logical reaction would have been to go into panic mode!

"What the heck was I thinking?" I remember recalling.

And yet I know myself, how ambitious I am, how I always feel like I want to accomplish so much.

It's only natural that when I realized the extent of my soul agreements, I would feel overwhelmed, overburdened and doubtful.

Maybe your life has been harder, too, and filled with more trials than your ego thought you could handle.

If you are reading this book, that means you're still alive. You are still making choices, both good and bad, which means you're still creating karma -- for both your benefit and your detriment.

Even so, just as you can clean up the basement of your house or calm an overactive mind, you can clean up your karma.

Here are some examples of karma you may need to clear:

Addiction
Emotional Starvation
Codependency
Deep-Seated Negative Experiences
Genetic Code Dysfunction
Heart Scars
Lost Soul Fragments
Negative Cords and Hooks
Negative Interference
Negative Self-Image
Parallel Universe Integration
Past Life Vows Preventing You from Giving or Receiving Love

Past Life Vows to Be a Caretaker
Past Life Vows Blocking Your Creativity
Past Life Vows of Poverty and Chastity
Past Life Vows of Vengeance and Revenge
Past Life Vows to Enslave or Be Enslaved
Past Life Vows Denying the Presence of God Within You
Past Life Vows Preventing the Personal Use of Healing Energies
Past Life Vows Denying Personal Responsibility
Past Life Vows of Sacrifice
Suffering

Addiction. You may not have thought of your addiction to drugs, alcohol, sex, exercise, overworking or any of the hundreds of other methods of self-medication as a karmic pattern.

Once you recognize the four levels you need to clear -- your thoughts, DNA, soul contract and the core of your soul -- you can appreciate how your previous efforts to release the patterns have proven so intractable. To free yourself from addiction requires very deep work indeed!

So often my clients have done a great job with inner work on one level but have not even been aware of other levels that when cleared can finally bless them with the freedom from addiction their souls crave.

Emotional Starvation. You may have a pattern deep inside your soul that keeps you from ever feeling complete emotional satisfaction.

This can occur when you've placed too much emphasis on certain aspects of your life -- for example, when you're overly focused on getting and keeping money at the expense of everything else.

Emotional starvation can keep you feeling lonely even when you're surrounded by loved ones and numerous friends.

It feels as though love is outside you, over there somewhere, rather than an energy you allow inside yourself to warm your heart and comfort your soul.

Codependency. You may be consciously or unconsciously processing other people's energy and emotions. I find the karma of codependency in everyone suffering from physical parasites (or worms). You have a predisposition to allow other people to eat your lunch, literally. The trouble is you can't take away and claim anybody else's soul lessons even if you wanted to do so. You can't do their life for them.

Processing other people's energy, emotions and karma is exhausting. When you let go and allow other people to live their lives the way their souls know best, you get a tremendous amount of your energy back.

Deep-Seated Negative Experiences. Just listening to the trauma many people have lived through can be hard. I will never forget a young man telling me about being raped by three men when his mother was late picking him up after a theater practice. (By the time he told his story, he was already an adult. Had he been under the age of 18, I would have legally been bound to report the story to the police.)

The man's parents didn't know about the rape, and he didn't want to tell them because he thought he was protecting his mother from shame and embarrassment. Unfortunately, his mother cut off our sessions to save money, and I couldn't tell her the actual reason he needed so much help.

The strongest of souls may have suffered from the deepest scars. Trust that there are no mistakes and that everything works out for your highest good.

Genetic Code Dysfunction. Because you are a member of the human race, you have cellular knowledge of how to be radiantly healthy. At the same time, our environment turns on and turns off certain genetic predispositions for illness. Your ancestors may have suffered from specific diseases, and you also bring forth the cellular memory of their pain and suffering.

You carry 50 percent of your mother's DNA and 50 percent of your father's DNA. You carry 25 percent of each grandmother's DNA and 25 percent of each grandfather's DNA. You would have to go back seven generations to get to a little more than 1 percent of your genetic code. By clearing karma through your DNA level, you can clear genetic code dysfunction and can call up the memory of perfect health.

Heart Scars. Healing from heart disease isn't necessarily just about eating better, lowering your stress and exercising regularly. The wounds you have experienced in this lifetime (or earlier) may have caused you to close off your heart to the unconditional love that sustains all of us. You may be punishing yourself for what you perceive to be mistakes or protecting yourself from being hurt again.

As you heal the karma of those heart scars, you restore your ability to love and be loved again, your depression lifts, and your blood pressure can normalize.

Lost Soul Fragments. In some shamanic traditions, this is called a soul retrieval. Let me explain how I see it.

Let's say you're driving a nice car. As you keep motoring along, you experience a series of minor accidents.

First, you lose a hubcap. Then a windshield wiper goes missing. Finally, your side rearview mirror gets knocked off.

In the same way, as we go through life, either by choice or circumstance, we may lose important aspects of ourselves.

For example, I went 18 years between my first and second books. I quite literally felt I had lost my inner author.

You may have set aside key aspects of who you really are in order to focus on surviving or supporting other family members. Through karmic clearing, you can call back aspects of your true self that you have lost in this or any other lifetime.

Negative Cords and Hooks. You may have allowed other people to hook into your energy. Lucy, age 60, had a mother, age 80, so demanding that she expected Lucy to drop everything and make her comfortable. Mom didn't like her nursing home and announced she should be allowed to move into Lucy's home with her husband.

Lucy was so hooked by her mother's energy she contracted a severe neurological disease to give herself an excuse not to meet the relocation demands.

Negative Interference. Often the negative interference we experience can be the result of sexism or racism. You may not be able to get ahead because of the negativity directed toward the group you belong to -- *e.g.*, women, Muslims, blacks, Mexicans, gays and transgender people.

Your soul transcends gender, your sexual orientation, a race or even a country. Prejudice and negative expectations hurt all the way to the level of your soul.

Negative Self-Image. You may be caught in the image of yourself from this or another lifetime. You may have made so many mistakes that you've come to believe you're a "bad" person. I sometimes joke, "Payback is hell! You must have been a mass murderer in a past lifetime."

Every lifetime and every day are chances to begin again.

As you learn to forgive yourself for past mistakes, you can let go of who you thought you were so you can become who your soul wants you to be.

Parallel Universe Integration. This is an interesting one. You may need to clear the karma of a parallel universe because your soul is literally living in two lifetimes simultaneously. This occurs most often when you haven't yet fully completed all your life's lessons before your soul starts another lifetime.

Parallel universe integration is a very common cause of exhaustion, spaciness and never quite feeling at home in your body. You're not all here because you literally aren't all here!

Past Life Vows Preventing You from Giving or Receiving Love. If you feel you're always unlucky in love, you may have taken vows in another lifetime agreeing not to give or receive unconditional love. Often the vows represent a form of self-sacrifice as you devoted your life to other causes.

Past Life Vows to Be a Caretaker. In another lifetime, you may have agreed to be the person serving others rather than someone receiving care. The pattern often will show up in your current life because you're constantly doing things for others and don't know how to let anyone do anything for you.

Past Life Vows Blocking Your Creativity. Writer's block

may have a root cause! In another lifetime, you may have agreed to focus on serving another purpose or to channel your own creativity for someone else's benefit.

When you clear your karma, you give yourself permission to say what you want to say, how you want to express it and in whatever form you think best. You give yourself permission to create from your soul, knowing the world needs your unique vision.

Past Life Vows of Poverty and Chastity. No matter how hard you try, you may find yourself without money or love. Turns out, you may have a soul agreement to stay poor and alone. In past lifetimes, many monks and nuns took vows of poverty and chastity upon entering their houses of spiritual protection and worship. No amount of relationship counseling will work until you clear these previous soul agreements.

Past Life Vows of Vengeance and Revenge. In another lifetime, either you, a family member or your tribe may have been attacked. You swore an oath of vengeance. Nowadays, you may find yourself in never-ending battles. Even if it appears you get what you think you want, the cycle of attack and revenge continues.

Past Life Vows to Enslave or Be a Slave. You may have agreed to own other people or be owned. In some parts of the world, human beings are still treated like property.

Even if you aren't an official slave, you may find yourself

working for practically nothing, never able to obtain true freedom.

If so, you may need to clear the karma of slavery. When you compassionately understand how millions of people are carrying the DNA of slaves, you can appreciate how many people continue to manifest that unfortunate reality.

Past Life Vows Denying Presence of God Within You. You may be suffering from the karma of identifying too much with material reality. Doubting the spiritual aspects of life is an honest position. Who hasn't questioned what it's all about anyway? But thinking you know there's nothing outside what can be quantified is another position entirely. If that's all there is -- just paying the rent and taking care of business-- you're likely suffering from a fatigue no degree of drugs or natural healing remedies can alleviate. If so, you have cut off the flow of divine intelligence and may find yourself constantly exhausted, distrustful of life and unable to access your soul guidance.

Past Life Vows Preventing Personal Use of Healing Energies. If you find yourself unable to heal, you may want to find out if you're suffering from this karma. If so, you will find yourself suffering from a seemingly incurable illness. Nobody can help you, and you can't do anything to heal others.

Past Life Vows Denying Personal Responsibility. As long as you continue to see others as perpetrators, you will view yourself as a victim. One of the many problems of staying in victim energy is that it keeps you in a disempowered state. Only when you take 100 percent responsibility for everything you have created do you begin to take your power back.

The tendency to blame others; the weather, the government, the bad guys, the evil in the world keeps you in the karma of denying personal responsibility. When you accept that everything that has ever happened in your life is, in fact, for your highest good, you can begin to overcome this karma.

Past Life Vows of Sacrifice. You may think it's noble to give away your time, money and personal energy. That is a common vow from past lives and one encouraged by many religious institutions.

You may have been taught you must sacrifice to get ahead -- not just spiritually but also in your career. But, what if you've been blessed in certain ways for your own benefit? What if so-called "getting ahead" could simply be a matter of setting your intention to experience something even better without having to encounter any misery to get there?

Suffering. As I wrote in my book *The Difference Between Pain and Suffering,* pain is the physical experience, while suffering is our emotional response.

Many people are actually addicted to suffering.

You may heal your broken ankle and then hurt your knee.

You may fix your ankle and knee and then break up with your boyfriend. You may be so caught up in the cycle of misery that you don’t even recognize what you're doing: creating one disaster after another and preventing yourself from experiencing the full joy available in life on earth.

Realize that "difficult" is the largest cult in the world! You don't have to take on everyone's suffering. What if you could be inspiring, uplifting instead? Instead of getting caught up in the karma of suffering, try to serve as a good example and be funny or insightful.

Chapter 6:
How to Clear Your Karma

"When the soul heals, the issues of the body disappear like they never happened."

- Pawan Mishra

As you read over the previous karma clearing to-do list, you may have recognized you have plenty to release. Here's how I clear karma:

Step One. Call in all your angels and spiritual guides for guidance and protection.

Step Two. Clear the energy in your space. I use this prayer:

Heavenly Father,
I call on the forces of nature to converge to balance all detrimental energies and increase all beneficial energies in this (room, space, home) for the benefit of all living beings. I ask that this be done in the name of Jesus Christ. Amen.

Step Three. Call in the team of angels collectively known as the Lords of Karma. Who are they?

The Lords of Karma are high-frequency individuals who have made a soul agreement to serve the planet. They may include angels and archangels, saints, enlightened beings and ascended masters.

You can think of them as referees in the game of life. They make and change the rules.

At this step, you're asking the enlightened beings to change the spiritual rules that have governed your own life.

Step Four. Ask the Lords of Karma for permission to clear a specific karma.

Even if you recognize you have lots of karma to let go of, you will want to clear one issue at a time so you can process the changes easily.

You may hear a "yes." If you use kinesiology or a pendulum for answers, you'll receive a "yes."

If you receive a "no" answer, continue with your current karma because there is still more for you to learn. It may not be the right time, or you may need additional resources to lift (or clear) what's actually going on.

Step Five. Once you receive a yes, ask the Lords of Karma if you can learn anything else mentally or emotionally from your pattern.

You may hear a "yes." If you use kinesiology or a pendulum for answers, you will receive a "yes." If so, pray and ask for guidance about what else you may need to learn.

You can then say this prayer:

Heavenly Father, I call on the Lords of Karma, all my angels and all my spiritual guides, to clear this karma from my mind. I ask that this be done in the name of Jesus Christ.

Thank you God, thank you God, thank you God.
Amen.

Afterwards, notice if there is anything you need to be, do or have to anchor this shift. When you anchor a shift, you bring the frequency of the healing into the present now in material reality. If you receive a "no" answer, more than likely there is nothing more for you to learn by continuing with your current karma.

Step Six. Ask the Lords of Karma if you are carrying the pattern from your ancestors. If so, then ask if it is being channeled through your mother's DNA, your father's DNA or both.

Next, go back through your ancestry and trace the pattern:

FIRST GENERATION: You
SECOND GENERATION: Mother/Father
THIRD GENERATION: Grandmother/Grandfather
FOURTH GENERATION: Great-Grandmother/Great-Grandfather
FIFTH GENERATION: Great- Great-Grandmother/Great- Great- Grandfather
SIXTH GENERATION: Great-Great-Great-Grandmother /Great-Great-Great-Grandfather

SEVENTH GENERATION: Great-Great-Great-Great Grandmother/Great-Great-Great-Great Grandfather

Keep going until you've identified all the ancestors with whom your pattern started. You may have to go back through seven generations or more.

Because 50 percent of your DNA comes from your father and the other 50 percent from your mother, each generation you go back in time gets split in half. Typically, you won't have to go back more than seven generations to clear a pattern all the way through your DNA.

As you identify the ancestors who carry the genetic tendency you're hoping to release, ask the Lords of Karma to clear the pattern all the way through your lineage. You can say this prayer:

Heavenly Father, I call on the Lords of Karma, all my angels and all my spiritual guides, to clear this karma all the way through my genetic programming and all the way through my ancestors. I ask that this be done in the name of Jesus Christ.

Thank you God, thank you God, thank you God.
Amen.

After you've said the prayer, notice if there is anything you need to be, do or have to anchor the shift.

Step Seven. Ask the Lords of Karma if you have any soul

agreements holding the pattern in place. As I've explained, there are three kinds of soul agreements:

1. You've agreed to help another soul.

2. Another soul agreed to help you.

3. Two souls agreed to help each other for their mutual benefit.

Even if your soul agreement is one-way, it's a sacred contract.

Once you identify what kind of soul contract you have and whom you are helping and/or who is helping you, ask the Lords of Karma for permission to complete it.

Especially if you've had an unpleasant interaction with someone, you want to be done with the pattern so that you don't repeat it with that person or someone else. You can say this prayer:

Heavenly Father, I call on the Lords of Karma, all my angels and all my spiritual guides, to complete this karmic contract with (name of person). I ask that this be done in the name of Jesus Christ.

Thank you God, thank you God, thank you God.
Amen.

After you've said the prayer, notice if there is anything you need to be, do or have to anchor the shift.

Step Eight. Ask the Lords of Karma to clear the pattern all the way through the core of your soul from the beginning of time to now. Because your soul has been around for a while -- going back many lifetimes -- you will want to clear it through the core of your soul.

You can say this prayer:

Heavenly Father, I call on the Lords of Karma, all my angels and spiritual guides, to clear this karma all the way through the core of my soul. I ask that this be done in the name of Jesus Christ.

Thank you God, thank you God, thank you God.
Amen.

After you've said the prayer, notice if there is anything you need to be, do or have to anchor the shift.

Step Nine. When you receive soul guidance that your healing is complete, thank the Lords of Karma and all of your angels and spiritual guides for their divine intervention.

Give thanks for your new way of being!

Chapter 7: Your List of Mistakes Will Only Get Longer, I Promise

"Life is just a chance to grow a soul."
- *A. Powell Davies*

Recently I was listening to a client in her 40s.

"I've made so many mistakes," she lamented.

Indeed, she had made an error of judgment that cost her $15,000.

"That's better than therapy," I observed. "You will never forget that one!"

As she was going over her long list of so-called mistakes, I interrupted her.

"How old are you?" I asked.

"I'm 45," she replied.

"Just wait until you are my age, 60. The list will only get longer!"

There are several ways to look at your list of so-called mistakes:

Some people have to learn by experience. Only the lucky

ones can take advice, read directions in a book or have someone in their family explain it to them. The rest of us are experiencing life in the do-it-yourself mode.

Mistakes create contrast. How would you know you don't look good in an orange shirt if you didn't make the mistake of wearing one in the first place? By doing things the wrong way, you learn what bad actually feels like so that you can make a better choice next time.

You expand your capacity to handle life. If everybody had to be perfect to get through life, we'd all be dead before we turned four years old. When you discover you can make a bad choice and live to tell the tale, you expand your capacity to tolerate the risk of being human. It's OK to look like a spastic monkey. It's OK to put your foot in your mouth, take a miserable job, marry the wrong person, give your kids bad directions, go left when you should have gone right or make many other common errors.

Once you realize you'll survive everything that happens to you until you don't, you can feel a lot more at ease.

Chapter 8:
The Cloud of Unknowing

"Love is the only way to reach God. Knowledge does not assist us."

- *Author Unknown, The Cloud of Unknowing*

One of the most common ways we humans try to maintain the illusion of control is by attempting to understand everything. "When I know better, I can do better" is often a truthful observation.

And yet when we finally understand that everything is happening on its own accord -- that conditions manifest when circumstances allow-- we can become more and more comfortable with the cloud of unknowing.

In the 14th century, an anonymous author wrote a book of Christian mysticism in Middle English called *The Cloud of Unknowing.*

This little book suggests the way to know God is to surrender your ego mind and accept the realm of the unknowing. By relinquishing the need to have all the answers, we can open ourselves up to have a direct experience with the divine rather than an intellectual understanding.

Having a gentle spirit doesn't necessarily mean showing courage, although it may be helpful. It also doesn't mean trust, although learning to trust the process of your life may lead to greater inner peace.

Having a gentle spirit means making peace with the cloud of unknowing. It means accepting that it's OK not to know what you're doing or where you're going, what your soul purpose is, why you made a mistake yesterday or how it's all going to work out.

As you accept the conditions of living in the cloud of unknowing, you let go and allow your soul to lead the way, past the sharp edges of your ego, into the light of unconditional acceptance for all that is.

By softening your vision, you allow yourself to see in the dark so much more clearly.

That is the essence of faith -- to become comfortable with the cloud of unknowing.

Chapter 9:
The Reason Why

"My soul can find no staircase to heaven unless it be through Earth's loveliness."

- *Michelangelo*

When I was about 17, I was traveling on a train to a new school. I didn't know anybody on the train.

I was dressed in a brand-new uniform that I thought was about as ugly as you could get. It featured a green skirt as thick as a blanket, a button-down shirt with a striped tie (like a boy would wear) and a cape that resembled something the Salvation Army might have handed out to the homeless.

Terribly nervous, I had never been to the new school and had no idea what to expect.

I was sitting next to a man intently reading a small tan pamphlet. When he stood up to get off the train, he handed the pamphlet to me.

It was called *The Reason Why*. The title was printed in big red letters, making it seem even more important. When I got to the school, I put the pamphlet in a wooden cigar box.

For the next 20 years, I took the box with me wherever I lived without ever opening the first page of the pamphlet.

"If things get really desperate," I would tell myself, "I'm going to read *The Reason Why.*"

Just knowing I had a pamphlet that promised to reveal *The Reason Why*, I managed to get through decades of life without needing an actual explanation.

Why did the school uniform need to be so ugly?

Why the hell did everything seem so difficult?

When was my life going to get any easier?

I decided deep inside that I didn't need to know why.

That is the essence of faith.

By continuing to walk without knowing what was in *The Reason Why,* I embraced the cloud of unknowing.

Book IV
The Soul Awakes

"When the ego dies, the soul awakes."
- Mahatma Gandhi

Chapter 1:
The Melancholy Healer

"Not everybody can heal under the light. Some need the darkness."

- *Akshay Vasu*

Like me, Shelley (not her real name) is a master healer. Her practice in the U.K. had grown to the point she had developed a clientele that came from far and wide.

Unfortunately, Shelley became so ill she had to shut her practice down. She called me for a reading. "I've always been looking for someone like me just to have someone else look into me," she explained.

Being a clairvoyant, Shelley had been able to see the negative spirit attachments afflicting her many clients.

"I take them off, and everybody gets better," she explained.

"You're right," I agreed.

For decades, I also have been removing negative spiritual entities and know how powerful the practice can be. By the way, I don't always tell people they've been cleared. Sometimes all they need to know is that they came to see me and now they feel better. Not everybody can handle understanding what actually just happened.

In fact, the first person I ever cleared of entities was a Catholic priest who had suffered severe depression and jaw pain for five years.

“Oh great,” I thought to myself when I figured out what was happening. “You’re going to tell a Catholic priest that he’s possessed.”

But I prayed for guidance and was told he could indeed handle the information.

“I know,” he told me.

“I respect your tradition,” I said to him. “Please go find someone who can clear it for you.”

When that didn't work, the priest returned. After the entity was cleared, all his pain and severe depression simply went away.

So, when Shelley told me about her practice, I completely understood.

Even though her clients got better, the work had been getting to her.

In fact, Shelley had been taking on her clients' karmas. As masterful as she was, she had been unwittingly processing their energies. Her energetic field hadn't been fully protected.

And most of all, Shelley felt saddened by what she saw. “It’s so painful for you,” I said to her.

“You can very clearly see what’s happening and the choices people are making. They are not conscious to the degree you are.

“They don’t see as clearly as you do that they are literally choosing between good and evil, making serious choices in their lives.

“You see it with dead clarity.

“They don’t see it at all.”

Chapter 2:
The Embattled Soul

"We repeat what we don't repair."

- Christine Langley-Obaugh

Mary Ellen thought of herself as a brilliant lawyer. While practicing law, going to court and defending cases, however, she somehow managed to live a double life as a drug addict.

In fact, Mary Ellen had been taking so many drugs (legal and illegal) that she was on what I would refer to as the Michael Jackson drug protocol -- a list so long you would have needed a Ph.D. in toxicology to figure out why the vast, poisonous cocktail hadn't killed her already.

Apparently, Mary Ellen's body wasn't happy with all the pills. Even though she was only in her late 30s, she had suffered a series of seizures.

Meanwhile, the domestic disturbances Mary Ellen had been having with her boyfriend became so violent the police were called to intervene on numerous occasions.

And once, while Mary Ellen was trying to score some cocaine, a Mexican family in Texas had kidnapped her, hoping to ransom her for money.

The darkness she faced was very real. "It's as if there has

been a battle for your very soul," I explained to Mary Ellen.

Every time she tried to get off one drug, another doctor would prescribe a new one. It was clear she wanted to be healthier because she longed to have a baby. But she couldn't slip out of her deep addictions.

Every time I thought Mary Ellen was ready to face herself, she would claim she was too busy with her law practice to do the inner work and deal with what was really bothering her.

On days when Mary Ellen looked good, she wanted to keep up appearances. On other days, when darkness fell, the terror of feeling what was deep inside came over her, and she could hardly get out of bed.

Chapter 3:
The Growling Trainer

"Some of the greatest battles will be fought within the silent chambers of your own soul."
- Ezra Taft Benson

Frederick was an unusual client because he already knew what was wrong with him before we even spoke. He just didn't know how to fix it.

Some years earlier, Frederick said, he lived through what he described as a horrible experience. A trusted mentor led him and a few others on what was billed as a shamanic journey. Over a two-day period, they took a combination of three psychedelic drugs -- ayahuasca, LSD and DMT.

"I almost died," Frederick told me. "It was a really bad trip. I felt cracked open and filled with dark energy. I was just broken, and it took me two years to get out of it."

Frederick knew he had a negative spirit attachment. His symptoms included shaking, convulsions and growling at random times of the day.

At times, he said his tongue would move like a lizard. "It feels like a reptilian energy," he reported.

He had other odd symptoms: "My body will get twisted when walking. My neck will get twisted. I feel burning sensations down my arm, head and neck.

"It feels sometimes like something is attached to the back of my head and neck and upper back."

In his public life, Frederick had become a much sought-after expert in nutrition, therapeutic exercise and body mechanics. His diet and workouts were beyond reproach.

Frederick had consulted with a number of healers to try to remove the entity, but "it keeps coming back," he lamented.

I explained that he hadn't been able to get rid of the negative entity completely because (1) the other healers hadn't repaired the huge tear in his energy field, and (2) he hadn't cleared his karma with the entity.

Think of the energy field as your skin, which protects your bones and internal organs. What would you feel like if you didn't have skin?

When there is a break in your energy field, you become hypersensitive to all kinds of frequencies and are susceptible to further negative spiritual attachments.

"I'm a nice person, but if I keep my front door open, anything can get in -- mice, raccoons or negative spirit attachments," I observed.

The tear in Frederick's energy field was really something to behold. It was the size of his torso, both front and back.

"Poor baby," I said to Frederick. "You win the prize. This is the biggest hole in an energy field I have ever seen."

Now keep in mind I was reading Frederick from afar as he lived in another city and we were working by phone. I couldn't see him in person -- I was just reading his soul.

I patched the hole in his energy field, explained to him what he needed to do to protect his energy on a daily basis, and performed a healing so that he could clear his karma with the entity.

"Clearing this entity is part of your soul path," I told Frederick. "When people have stuff going on at the soul level, that dictates everything.

"You can medicate it -- with natural supplements or drugs -- but that's still not going to heal what's going on unless you work at the soul level.

"You now have a much greater appreciation of what can be going on with people. Not everybody has negative spirit attachments, but it's what's going on at the soul level that is what is really going on."

Chapter 4:
How to Keep Your Shadow from Ruining Your Life

"One does not become enlightened by imagining figures of light, but by making the darkness conscious."

- Carl Jung

Although you may want to be guided by your soul, you may find the unknown, dark side of your personality getting in the way.

If I were to describe my work as a medical intuitive healer, I would say it's like reading a book.

I have to read the words on the page.

Not the words I think are written.

Not the glamorous words the author wants other people to see.

But what is actually there.

The great psychologist Carl Jung wrote at length about the personality's unconscious aspects. "Until you make the unconscious conscious, it will direct your life, and you will call it fate," he said.

It's easy to get fooled by the shadow -- both your own and other people's shadows.

What is your shadow? It's the negative aspects of your ego self that you've been hiding from yourself and others.

Everybody has a shadow, including you.

Here are a few methods I've learned to help you keep the shadow from ruining your life:

Circle with an X

One simple energy tool comes from Therapeutic Energy Kinesiology (TEK). When I'm working with clients in person, I begin by checking numerous energy points including your shadow point.

Your shadow point is an energy center on your left temple, at the side of your left eye.

If I am muscle-testing the shadow point and discover your shadow to be in charge, I'll simply draw a circle over the point with an X through it. That tells your shadow to take a hike so I can communicate with your soul.

If you want your soul to be in charge, simply draw a circle with an X over your left temple.

Recognize Your Own Archetypes

"Knowing your own darkness is the best method for dealing with the darknesses of other people," Carl Jung said.

“The most dangerous psychological mistake is the projection of the shadow onto others: This is the root of almost all conflicts.”

In my office I have a long list of archetypes that may be running your show.

Medical intuitive Carolyn Myss has written at length about archetypes and created a deck of 80 possible characters. For starters, everybody has an Inner Child, Victim, Prostitute and Saboteur.

Some of your archetypes may empower you to feel sexy, powerful, glamorous or important. You may even fool yourself into believing you are your archetype or that your archetype is your soul purpose. After all, who doesn’t have fun being the King, the Queen, the Damsel in Distress, the Visionary, the Poet or the Rebel?

Here is how I like to explain it: If you go down to the theater and try out for the part of Blanche Dubois in *A Streetcar Named Desire*, you put on the costume and speak the lines, but you aren’t actually Blanche. You're playing a role.

Other people may even tell you that you're the very best Blanche Dubois they have ever seen. You may have a great time being Blanche. But, at the end of the day, you should hang up the dress and stop talking that way.

You need to be you.

As much as possible, you want your soul to be in charge.

That's because you are a soul who has a body. Your soul has a mission to complete in this lifetime. When you listen to your soul, you can be guided from within to all that leads to your greater good.

Allowing your shadow to rule is the root of all self-destruction.

By learning to recognize when your own archetypes are taking over, it's easier to observe when other people are living from their shadow selves.

When you can see your own faults as well as your strengths, you can develop a compassionate view of not only yourself but all others.

"Anyone who perceives his shadow and his light simultaneously sees himself from two sides and thus gets in the middle," Jung explained.

Visualize Yourself in a Holy Temple

Recently I was consulted by a woman who had been conned out of $100,000. In our first session, I was able to identify that the man who convinced her to give him the money in exchange for a job in his company was not in integrity.

My client wanted to give him a piece of her mind, but both

her lawyer and I advised her to get out of the situation as quickly as possible.

“When you meet a bear in the woods, you don’t stand there and scold him that he’s big, hairy and ugly,” I explained. “You get out of there as quickly as possible.”

Unfortunately, the truth is there are people in the world whose sole aim is to separate you from your money, good intentions, brilliant ideas and everything else you had hoped to use for a higher purpose.

They know the game they're playing and do everything in their power to hide who they are and what they're really up to.

When you're wanting to see another person's shadow, visualize both yourself and the other person in a Holy Temple. Shut your eyes and imagine you're in God’s House.

Say a prayer and call in all your angels and spiritual guides. Ask for assistance to be shown who is really there and what is actually happening.

You could say this prayer:

Heavenly Father,

I call on all my angels and my spiritual guides. I ask for divine assistance in seeing the truth of this situation. Please show me the truth in ways so clear that even I can understand. Give me permission to see the shadow and the light, to see the whole picture for the highest good of all.

I ask that this be done in the name of Jesus Christ.

Thank you God, thank you God, thank you God.
Amen.

Then imagine yourself playing a game of hide-and-seek.

Look behind every column in the church.

Set your intention to see the shadow of the other person.

See what you see. Hear what you hear.

Then use that information to guide your true path.

The only way to live in the light is by constantly knowing where your shadow is and being aware of other people's shadows.

Chapter 5: Negative Spiritual Energy, an Overlooked Aspect of Poor Health

"Look at how a single candle can both defy and define the darkness."

- *Anne Frank*

You may be taking medication, following a thorough homeopathic regimen, exercising regularly, praying and meditating twice a day, repeating affirmations and thinking as positively as you can but feel like you are getting nowhere.

It's possible one minor detail is holding you back: negative spiritual energy.

What is negative spiritual energy? On a scale of angelic to demonic, it's all about frequency, energy and intention.

If you have studied the work of David Hawkins, M.D., you may be familiar with his famous scale of consciousness, from zero to 1,000. You can think of the frequencies as levels of energy.

Everything below 200 is not in integrity and is destructive to life. Several emergency emotions include shame (20), guilt (30), apathy (50), grief (75), fear (100), desire (125), anger (150), and pride (175).

Each frequency has physical issues associated with it. For

example, anger damages your liver and gallbladder. Grief affects your lungs.

In so many ways, the sub-200 emotions are the levels of hell on earth.

Because you're human, you may feel any or all of the emergency emotions from time to time. The trick is to avoid getting stuck in them or trapped in the frequency of the energy field they create.

Here is another way to understand Hawkins' level of consciousness scale.

Maybe you went to college. You got a B in Spanish and an F in physics. Overall, you earned a grade point average (GPA).

Similarly, your level of consciousness is a composite of your view of God, your view of life, your primary emotions and the process of spiritual ascension you are undergoing.

I want all my clients to reach a level of at least 310, which is willingness. When you're willing to get better, you are open to whatever it takes to heal.

If you aren't quite up to willingness yet, I will do an in-depth healing to clear the blocks, congestion, resistance or interference so you can eventually be the very best you can be.

Once you reach willingness, the next major turning points are reason (400), love (500) and unconditional love (540). Most certified healers I know operate in the frequency of love because it is the most powerful healing frequency in the world.

Hawkins writes that only four-tenths of one percent of all humans ever reach a level of consciousness of 500 or above. Rarer still is enlightenment (600).

The levels above 600 are achieved only by advanced spiritual sages. Jesus and Buddha lived at 1,000, making them powerful avatars who influenced the lives of billions of people who came after them.

Angels exist at frequencies above 1,000.

According to Hawkins, an archangel's frequency is at 50,000, making a single encounter with an angel or archangel a permanently life-altering experience.

When you come to the understanding that it's all one energy, that it's all good and that it's all God, there is nothing to fear.

There's salt, and there's pepper. Neither one is bad nor good.

There's yin and there's yang energies. Both are helpful, both life-supporting.

Negative spiritual energies include frequencies that drag down your life force.

So in terms of angelic vs. demonic, it's just a question of focus. Set your intention to attune yourself to the highest and best vibrations, and you'll be sure to experience radiant health and happiness.

Chapter 6:
How to Clear Negative Spiritual Energies

"My deepest me is God."
- St. Catherine of Genoa

Clearing negative spiritual energy may be one of the simplest, most powerful ways to shift what's going on with your total well-being. Here's how to do it:

Step One. Clear the energy of your space. Many people burn sage. I use this prayer:

Heavenly Father,
I call on the forces of nature to converge to balance all detrimental energies and increase all beneficial energies in this (room, space, home) for the benefit of all living beings. I ask that this be done in the name of Jesus Christ. Amen.

A couple of comments about the prayer:

First, although I frequently recommend flower essences and diffuse essential oils and often burn sage in my healing room, your best approach is to use pure energy to clear energy.

Second, prayer is one of the most powerful tools you have at your disposal.

In the space-clearing prayer, you ask to balance the

detrimental energies.

You ask to increase the beneficial energies to turn up the volume, so to speak, on all frequencies that are life-supporting.

I grew up in the Christian tradition, so I call on the name of Jesus. You may call on other spiritual guides such as angels, archangels, ascended masters and your own team of angels.

As you say the prayer, point your dominant hand to a corner of the room. To clear the energy, move your hand in a counterclockwise direction.

To infuse energy, move your hand in a clockwise direction.

As you say the prayer, move your hand in a counterclockwise direction.

Visualize a miniature cyclone of energy moving through the room and clearing out the detrimental energies.

It's important to clear the energy in any room before you do healing work so that you set the proper environment for your client and you to prosper.

Step Two. Clear your shadow. When you do this work, you want your soul to be in charge.

As I have explained, there's an energy center on your left temple, next to your left eyebrow, called the shadow point.

Draw a circle with your finger around the point. Then draw an X through the circle.

This energy technique allows you to set your shadow aside.

Step Three. Call in all your angels and spiritual guides.

I do this with a prayer:

Heavenly Father,

I call on all my angels and all my spiritual guides. I ask them to be with me, to guide me, to uplift me and to work through me now for the highest good of all. I ask that this be done in the name of Jesus Christ. Amen.

Step Four. Determine whether any negative spiritual entities are attached to the person.

If you are clairvoyant, you'll see the entities are connected to the person's energy field.

If you use kinesiology, the hand mode for negative spiritual energies is your thumb to the middle digit of the inside of your little finger. If you hold this hand mode and it tests strong, the person you are testing has a negative spirit attachment.

Optional: It isn't necessary to determine what kind of negative spiritual energy you're confronting, but sometimes it can be helpful to find out. Examples include:

Black Magic
Earthbound Entities
Emotional Turmoil Entities
Fear Entities
Gloom, Doom and Disaster
Gray Entities
Negative Spirit Attachments
Poltergeists
Satanic Entities

Step Five. Determine the emotions that the negative spiritual entities have been causing. I usually find they are causing people to experience a myriad of negative emotions, including depression, anxiety, confusion, self-destructive thoughts, hopelessness, morbid ideas and more.

Step Six. While the person being cleared is either lying or sitting down, hold her forehead with one hand while holding the back of her head with the other hand. This simple energy-healing technique allows the individual to release stress at a deep level.

While holding the person's forehead, have the person repeat after you:

I now joyfully release all negative spiritual energies that have made me feel (list the emotions you found here) from my past, in the present and for the future.

The person should repeat the affirmation at least three times.

Step Seven. Fill the void. Now that the attachment is gone, you can fill the energy field with beneficial energies.

Bring your thumb together with your little finger and ring finger, creating a hand mode in kinesiology that allows access to the spiritual realm. Then, tap a big circle around your ears to activate the acupuncture points.

While tapping around the ears, you should repeat the following affirmation:

I allow God to fill the empty void with love, joy, peace, patience, kindness, goodness, tolerance and self-control.

To activate all parts of your brain, repeat the affirmation, and move your eyes:

UP
DOWN
RIGHT
LEFT

Then, with your eyes closed, continue to repeat the affirmation, and moves your eyes:

UP
DOWN
RIGHT
LEFT

Step Eight: Check for holes in the energy field. Think of your energy field like a grid with both vertical and horizontal lines.

First, identify the rows and columns with holes.

Second, say a prayer, and channel healing energy to patch the holes. I am a Reiki master so I usually rely on Reiki healing energy for that purpose. Essential oils also may help, depending upon the person. Here is the prayer I use:

Heavenly Father, I call on all my angels and spiritual guides and all of (name of person's) angels and spiritual guides. I ask that the highest healing frequencies flow through me to patch the holes for the benefit of (name of person). I ask that the holes be filled with love, light and forgiveness. I ask that this be done in the name of Jesus Christ. Thank you God, thank you God, thank you God. Amen.

Third (optional), ask for guidance if the person needs to complete her karma with the negative spirit attachment. If so, you can use the karmic clearing process I described in Book III.

Step Nine: Clear the energy in your space again. Once the process is complete, repeat step one to release any and all negative energies that remain behind.

The person may now go home and rest.

I frequently encourage clients to use the space-clearing prayer in their home afterwards in case they had picked up anything from the environment.

Another suggestion is for the client to take a bath with equal parts Epsom salts and baking soda. One cup of each in a regular size bathtub is sufficient.

The bath clears your energy field and restores balance to your mind-body system after deep energy healing.

Essential oil of rosemary also clears negative spiritual energy. You can add a few drops to the bath.

Chapter 7:
Connect to God's Grace

"If I am not in God's grace, may God put me there; and if I am, may God so keep me there."
- *Joan of Arc*

When I was studying medical intuition, one of the most important things I was taught to do was to connect every aspect of myself to God.

To access the most accurate information, we paradoxically must push our ego mind out of the way. The rule is, "Show up and get out of your own way."

Why is that so important?

Our ego mind thinks we know what we know. For example, I have 26 years of full-time experience and training in natural healing. I have studied an enormous amount of information, learned from many top-notch teachers all over the world and practiced with clients both in person and remotely in North America, South America, Europe, Asia and Africa.

But no matter how much I have studied or practiced, there is a limit to what I can personally know.

My ego is finite.

I am smart enough to know that despite my many years of

training and experience, I don't actually know anything.

When we set our intention to connect every aspect of ourselves to the divine, we allow God to guide us on every level. We can become a channel and let ourselves be divinely led.

It takes great humility to recognize the absolute truth: "I don't know anything."

Even the highly trained mind can sometimes interfere with divine guidance.

Worries.

Wanting to be right.

Wanting to fix things.

Having a bad day.

Even being exhausted -- all these aspects of the ego can throw shade on the truth.

In adopting a humble and prayerful approach to my work and life itself, I allow myself to be guided to do what is best for me and my clients and communicate the information in a way that is helpful and useful.

When you connect every part of yourself to God, you can know whatever it is you need to know.

I begin every day with prayer, breathwork and meditation. My inner habit of prayer continues all day long.

I use the Lord’s Prayer as an attunement and repeat it until I can say every word smoothly and easily.

If I stumble over the words, I know I am out of alignment and start over from the beginning until I can repeat the prayer all the way correctly.

I couldn't even tell you how many prayers I say to myself throughout any given day. It’s simply part of the job, part of the attitude, part of how I do what I do.

Recently, someone gave me what I considered to be the worst possible insult: She said she didn't think I was a “traditional Christian.”

I go to church. I pray all day long. I have written books full of prayers.

The comment hurt. I felt she didn’t see who I am, how I approach my life and work or what I’m all about.

Just as a surgeon has a scalpel and a violinist has a violin and a bow, we all have tools to empower us to do what we do.

Whether you're wanting to improve your ability to receive soul guidance or to know and experience that everything is actually in divine order, you may find connecting to God extremely helpful. Here are some ways to do so:

Meditate
Repeat the Lord's Prayer
Pray for Guidance
Chant
Repeat Mantras
Sit in Silence
Read Sacred Texts
Call on Angels and Archangels
Give Gratitude to God for All You Have Received
Count Your Blessings
Set Your Intention to Serve God for the Highest Good.

In other words, show up and get your ego out of the way. When you can do that, you will experience less stress and enjoy the miracles of synchronicity.

What is healing? Healing happens when you allow yourself to be divinely guided to all that is truly helpful.

Chapter 8: Are You Having a Dark Night of the Soul or a Breakdown to a Breakthrough?

"You are unfolding in divine order."
- *Wayne Dyer*

One day a long-term client named Jan (not her real name) called me up and announced, "I'm having a nervous breakdown."

Now the term "nervous breakdown" implies you've lost control somehow or that whatever happens to be occurring might be really, really bad.

As Jan and I worked together, I was able to reframe what was happening.

"I don't think you are actually having a nervous breakdown," I observed. "I think you are breaking down to a breakthrough."

Although Jan had accomplished many goals in life -- raising children, creating a successful business -- she had never totally focused on being happy.

"I don't think you are a naturally depressed person," I said.

"You have just never figured out what your soul needs to be happy."

Sometimes our ego gets so set in its ways that the only way to allow shifts to occur is by breaking down old structures.

A breakdown to a breakthrough may occur after many seemingly unpleasant circumstances:

Death of a Loved One
Divorce
Major Illness
Loss of a Child
Loss of a Job
Bankruptcy
Emotional Meltdown
Financial Ruin
Going to Jail
Major Lawsuit
House Fire
Auto Accident

In other words, whatever you thought you once had going for you suddenly stops working.

Whenever you're having an actual what-the-heck moment in your life, it's important to ask yourself if what is happening is not in fact a breakthrough.

If you were to remain totally comfortable at all times, you might never be motivated to take the steps necessary to live a better life.

Recently I was interviewing a gentleman from Canada named Bob (not his real name) who uses iboga, the strongest plant medicine in the world, in ceremonies in the tradition of the Bwiti people of Africa.

Iboga is grown in West Central Africa. It is native to Gabon and used in rites of passage ceremonies when people are making a major transition.

Africa, Bob explained, is a harsh place. In the West, we're used to being soft, to feeling comfortable most if not all of the time.

Sometimes the harshest medicine is required to wake us up into a new dimension.

During an iboga ceremony, you may experience visions for up to 30 hours. Meanwhile, your body is purging at the deepest levels. You may be throwing up for almost as long as your soul shows you the visions you need to see.

It's a juxtaposition that we in the West aren't yet comfortable with -- the uncomfortable shift into deep spiritual understanding.

Your ego may be so resistant to knowing the truth that your soul has to set up a major life event to get your attention.

Next time you think you're absolutely losing it, pause for a moment and ask yourself: Am I breaking down the old structures of my life so that I can break through to the next level?

In astrology, when you go through the Saturn period, all the old structures -- even ones that appeared to be working for you -- get broken down to make way for the new.

You often feel alone and frequently go through a dark night of the soul experienced as severe depression. In those circumstances, no medication -- natural or prescription -- can touch what's really going on.

If you medicate your way through the experience, you may miss the point that during a dark night of the soul, you're supposed to be letting go at the deepest levels.

The harder you cling to what no longer works, the more pain and suffering you experience.

Give yourself permission to break down what no longer works so that you can break through to the next highest vibration!

Book V
Removing Barriers Against Love

"Your task is not to seek for love, but merely to seek and find all the barriers within yourself that you have built against it."

- Rumi

Chapter 1:
The Awakening of Marcus

"Keep looking for your voice. You will find it."
- Aretha Franklin

For most of his life, Marcus had felt overlooked. While growing up as the child of a single mother, he had shuffled around with his brothers and sisters, never excelling in school.

Shortly before his 40th birthday, Marcus felt the call to make something of himself although he wasn't sure what that was.

Marcus had been living with his girlfriend and young daughter and working as a welder.

Life surely had been passing him by, he felt. So he booked a trip to a spiritual retreat.

I was asked to do a medical intuitive reading for Marcus before he arrived so the people there would know how best to help him.

When I started the reading, my heart leapt with joy. "This morning, I woke up and my angels were chattering away to me about you," I wrote to Marcus.

"I felt so excited to do your reading. It's now 5:36 a.m., and I have no choice but to start writing down some of what my angels are saying to me about you.

"I love the early morning -- it's my favorite time of day -- and typically I wake up and start praying. I did get in a few prayers, but my angels are so excited to speak to you through me that this sacred time of my day is devoted to you and all that you need to begin to know, realize and learn about yourself.

"You have only thought you have wasted your life," I wrote to Marcus.

"You are now waking up to who you are.

"You are not a 'whatever.'

"You are recognizing you are a soul who matters.

"Study the life of plants," I suggested.

My most amazing, rare, endangered fairy orchid can look ugly for years. Then one day a bud will form.

"You haven't been wasting your life. You have been rooting -- grounding yourself into your culture, rooting yourself so that you can flower into the soul you are."

I told Marcus that I saw him in a community leadership role. I encouraged him to read books about servant leadership and find people he admired.

“You are waking up to your full power as a natural leader," I said. “You are waking up to your soul purpose.”

I encouraged Marcus to forgive himself for all the years he thought he had wasted.

You are never *not* on your spiritual path.

Sometimes it just feels like you are moving slowly!

Marcus wrote me back to say he had wept when he received my reading. He felt so thankful that someone else could see who he is and had affirmed him.

Chapter 2:
Not Your First Choice of Parents

"You've got to get up every morning with a smile on your face and show the world all the love in your heart."
- Carole King

Sally reached out to me for a medical intuitive reading because she felt so exhausted. She had been reading my book *Unlimited Energy Now* and thought I might be able to offer some insight.

As I tuned into Sally, I didn't begin by discussing proper rest or juicing or by identifying chronic infections that typically cause fatigue like Epstein-Barr virus.

I knew I needed to head straight for the soul level.

"You need to create a spiritual family," I advised Sally.

"That makes sense," Sally replied, "because mine sucks."

Often in life, we didn't get the biological father, mother, sister, brother, aunts or uncles we might have preferred. But there is no such thing as a vacuum in the universe.

God is always providing for us every moment of every day.

While you may not have been born into the ideal family of origin, you can pray and ask God to send you the spiritual mother, father, brother, sister, aunts or uncles your soul craves and that you actually need.

Look around.

Often those people are already in your life.

They may not be blood relatives, but on the soul level, they are your tribe. They can give you the unconditional love your soul needs, no strings attached.

You, in return, can love them back.

You can fill each other's hearts with the love everybody needs so badly.

As I went further into the reading, I pointed out that Sally was wasting 80 to 85 percent of her personal energy trying to fix things with her parents. "There's nothing to fix," I explained.

Sally's birth parents had given her a body and blessed her with the opportunity to be born in this lifetime. Even though we may want more, sometimes that is actually enough.

It was up to Sally to find her tribe -- the people who could really understand and support her.

She wasn't anything like her parents and never would be. That wasn't their fault, and it certainly wasn't her fault either.

“When you can move into unconditional acceptance of who your parents are, you will no longer be so exhausted.”

Chapter 3:
Panda Power Animal Awaits the Birth

"Being born on earth is the highest honor and greatest privilege. To be alive as human beings gives us the chance to pull off exquisite and Herculean feats of magic that are not possible in nirvana or heaven or any other so-called paradise, higher dimension, or better place. Being alive right now is the greatest gift I got from God."

\- *Rob Brezsny*

Elise, a lawyer and accountant, had worked since she was 13 years old. Even though she and her husband ran a successful business together, she felt something was missing in her life.

She longed for a child.

Elise had worked with medical doctors for five years, but her previous attempts to start a pregnancy had been expensive, painful, humiliating and ultimately unsuccessful.

Hearing that I had helped other women to overcome infertility, Elise began to work with me to clear her blocks to conceiving and carrying the child she wanted so badly.

At last, Elise finally conceived. She and her husband could barely contain their excitement.

But alas, when she went back to her doctor a few weeks

later, he told her he could find no heartbeat and that she had lost her child.

Desperate not to lose faith, Elise reached out me for a session. I led her on a soul journey to meet her unborn child.

When Elise arrived in the spirit world, she discovered that many, many souls were eagerly waiting to be born. As she communicated with each soul, a peace came over her like she had never felt before.

"It will be OK whatever it is, whether it's a girl, whether it's a boy," she concluded.

The following week, Elise went back to her doctor, who revealed he had made a mistake.

Her baby was, in fact, still alive, and her pregnancy continued.

On the morning Elise was preparing to give birth, the soul of her soon-to-be-born little boy came to me in a dream. He told me his power animal is a panda bear, and he showed me a vision of a baby panda high up in a tree, all fluffy, cute and adorable.

"I've been waiting," the baby's soul explained to me.

Although Elise had felt her miracle would never happen, the soul of her unborn baby had been ready and waiting for quite some time.

Chapter 4:
Waiting to Lose a Soul Mate

"Giving someone a piece of your soul is better than giving a piece of your heart. Because souls are eternal."
- Helen Boswell

Bob and Mary had been married for more than 30 years. Their partnership had been so rewarding that they had rarely spent much free time with friends.

"To have found the love of your life, that's enough," Mary told me.

After a series of heart attacks, Bob became less and less of himself.

The intimacy they both enjoyed so much was no longer possible.

A series of strokes left Bob unable to work. He stayed home and wandered about the house while Mary continued to go into the office, serving as not only the provider but also caretaker, cook, accountant and more.

Being a highly capable person, Mary wasn't bothered too much about taking care of all the responsibilities. Instead, it was the loneliness.

Even though Mary couldn't tell anyone else, she confessed to me that it might be easier for her if Bob passed away.

He was there but not actually there.

Mary no longer had a friend to hang out with, a lover to love, an adventurer to travel with.

“What’s he doing?” she asked me.

When I looked, I saw Bob's soul sitting in a circle, almost like a shamanic circle or a council of elders.

“He’s not doing anything,” I replied.

A few years passed.

While Mary was taking care of Bob and working full-time, she also managed to sell their old home and move into a new place closer to her daughters. He sat in the living room of their new home on days when he didn't attend an elder care program for patients with dementia.

Mary took care of the new home, painting the walls the colors she liked and setting up the extra bedrooms for their children and grandchildren to come and visit.

Meanwhile, Bob appeared to be doing practically nothing. And then one day, just as Mary had finally gotten her new home just like she liked it, he passed away.

“I see it now,” Mary told me later.

“Bob wanted to see where I was going. He wanted to make

sure that I’m going to be OK.”

Even though it appeared Bob had been doing nothing, his soul had been protecting Mary, watching out for her and waiting until he knew she was in fact OK

.

Spirit never misses a beat.

When true love loves, the bond persists past time and eternity.

Chapter 5:
Prayer to Archangel Michael

"The guardian angels of life sometimes fly so high as to be beyond our sight, but they are always looking down upon us."

- *Jean Paul*

As I prepared to write *Reading the Soul,* I asked for guidance one day and was told that Archangel Michael would be assisting me. That was an unusual occurrence, even for me.

I have written nine other books, and at no time was I ever told that an angel, much less an archangel, would be assisting my writing.

Archangel Michael, for those of you who haven't spent time getting to know him before now, is known as a healing angel and a leader of God's armies against the forces of evil.

Every morning as I was writing this book, I meditated on Archangel Michael. I visualized his shining white sword and shield of protection and the cobalt blue light of his presence surrounding me.

I waited patiently but was told he would not speak to me personally but rather through the words of this book.

I say a special prayer now in gratitude to Archangel

Michael and for the protection, guidance and upliftment to you who have read these words that he helped me to write:

Archangel Michael,

Thank you for your guidance, your unconditional love and your protection.

Please bless this reader now so that they know who they are as a soul.

Help them to see beyond earthly illusions to the truth of who they really are, why they are really here and all the unconditional love that surrounds them.

Please uplift their hearts.

Give them the courage to take up their soul purpose in this lifetime.

I ask that this be done in the name of Jesus Christ.

Thank you Archangel Michael, thank you, thank you.

Amen.

About the Cover

I first acquired my Brassolaeliocattleya Greenworth in October 2011 from the Atlanta Botanical Garden.

Because it was just a bud at the time, I wasn't sure what color it would turn out to be.

I placed the cattleya orchid in a sunny window of my healing room and waited patiently for the surprise.

For the past eight years, this chartreuse cattleya has been a constant source of delight for me and my clients, blooming about twice a year and filling the room with an indescribable perfume.

Orchids are the most evolved flowers on the face of the earth.

My favorite orchid, this Brassolaeliocattleya Greenworth, fulfills its soul purpose of radiating beauty and uplifting and delighting everyone who beholds it.

Cover design by RamaJon Cogan.

About the Author, Catherine Carrigan

Catherine Carrigan is a medical intuitive healer, Amazon No. 1 bestselling author and host of the Natural Healing Show for U.K. Health Radio.

She empowers her clients to alleviate pain and suffering through a wide range of natural healing methods.

You can connect with her on Facebook at https://www.facebook.com/catherinecarriganauthor

Follow her on Twitter at https://twitter.com/CSCarrigan

Read her blog at www.catherinecarrigan.com

Check out her websites at www.catherinecarrigan.com and www.unlimitedenergynow.com

Connect with her on LinkedIn at: www.linkedin.com/in/catherinecarrigan/

Keep up with news about her books at: https://www.goodreads.com/author/show/638831.Catherin e_Carrigan

Sign up for her newsletter at: http://bit.ly/1C4CFOC

You can read testimonials from her clients here:
http://catherinecarrigan.com/testimonials/

Training in Fitness

- Certified Personal Fitness Trainer: A.C.E. certified in Personal Fitness Training
- Corrective High-Performance Exercise Kinesiologist (C.H.E.K) Practitioner, Level I: C.H.E.K. Institute.
- Certified Group Exercise Instructor: A.C.E. certified in Group Exercise
- A.C.E. Specialty Recognitions: Strength Training and Mind-Body Fitness
- Exercise Coach, C.H.E.K. Institute
- Certified Yoga Teacher: 500-hour Yoga Teacher through Lighten Up Yoga; six 200-hour certifications through Integrative Yoga Therapy, the White Lotus Foundation, and the Atlanta Yoga Fellowship, Lighten Up Yoga and Erich Schiffmann teacher training (twice)
- Practitioner of qi gong, Chinese martial arts
- Certified Older Adult Fitness Trainer through the American Institute of Fitness Educators

Training in Nutrition

- Food Healing Level II Facilitator
- Holistic Lifestyle Coach though the C.H.E.K. Institute, Level 3
- Certified Sports Nutritionist through the American Aerobics Association International/International Sports Medicine Association
- Author, *Healing Depression: A Holistic Guide* (New York: Marlowe and Co., 1999), a book discussing nutrition and lifestyle to heal depression without drugs
- Schwarzbein Practitioner though Dr. Diana Schwarzbein, an expert in balancing hormones naturally

Training in Healing

- Specialized Kinesiology and Life Coaching through Sue Maes of London, Ontario, Canada
- Self-Empowerment Technology Practitioner
- Brain Gym, Vision Circles and Brain Organization instructor through the Educational Kinesiology Foundation
- Certified Touch for Health Practitioner

- Thai Yoga Body Therapy
- Flower Essence Practitioner
- Reiki Master, Usui Tradition
- Life Coaching through Sue Maes' Mastering Your Knowledge Mentorship Program and Peak Potentials
- Therapeutic Energy Kinesiology (TEK)
- Medical Intuitive Readings and Quantum Healing

Other Training

- Health and fitness columnist
- Playwright of 12 plays, including three produced in New York City
- Past spokesperson for the Depression Wellness Network
- Phi Beta Kappa graduate of Brown University
- Former national spokesperson for Johnson & Johnson
- Owner and co-host, Total Fitness Radio Show
- Author of *Healing Depression: A Holistic Guide*
- Author of the Amazon No. 1 best seller *What Is Healing? Awaken Your Intuitive Power for Health and Happiness*

- Author of the Amazon No. 1 best seller, *Unlimited Energy Now*
- Author of the Amazon No. 1 best seller, *Banish the Blues Now*
- Author of *What Is Social Media Today? Get Ready to Win the Game of Social Media*
- Author of the Amazon No. 1 best seller, *What Is Social Media Today? Hashtags, Keywords and You, Oh My!*
- Author of the Amazon No. 1 best seller, *The Difference Between Pain and Suffering*
- Author of the Amazon No. 1 best seller, *The Little Book of Breathwork*
- Author of the Amazon No. 1 best seller, *Unlimited Intuition Now*

Acknowledgments

I would like to thank all those without whose wisdom and generosity this book would not be possible. For my mentor in healing, Sue Maes; For Kathryn Ravenwood, for her past life regression work; For Darin McBratney, for hiring me to do medical intuitive readings for the Global Nurture Project; for my Reiki master teacher, William Rand; For my editor, Tony Kessler; For cover design and formatting, RamaJon Cogan; For Amazon marketing, Denise Cassino; For audiobook producer Mike Gustin; For narrator Holly Parsons and most especially for my grandmother Mae Nunnally Schulze, who awakened me to the world of the wondrous by first hypnotizing me as a child.

Other books and bestsellers from Catherine

THE DIFFERENCE
between
PAIN and SUFFERING
CATHERINE CARRIGAN

- Overcome your pain and suffering the natural way.

- Medical intuitive healer Catherine Carrigan shows you how.

- Discover drug-free secrets from yoga, Reiki, the world's

- Healthiest foods, energy healing and holistic alternative medicine

- With photographs and exercises that really work.

What is
HEALING?
AMAZON
#1
BESTSELLER
Awaken Your
Intuitive Power for
Health and Happiness
CATHERINE
CARRIGAN

About *What Is Healing? Awaken Your Intuitive Power for Health and Happiness*

In this book, you will:

- Learn how unconditional love can awaken your intuitive gifts.
- Reveal how to open your heart to access your highest intelligence.
- Uncover how to communicate with your angels and spiritual guides.
- Awaken your own psychic abilities.
- Identify the key aspects of a medical intuitive reading.
- Discern how addiction to staying sick can keep you from healing.
- Reveal the blessing behind a mental or physical breakdown.
- Grasp the four key difficulties that lead to health problems.
- Empower your own spiritual growth.

UNLIMITED
ENERGY
NOW
AMAZON
#1
BESTSELLER
CATHERINE
CARRIGAN

About *Unlimited Energy Now*

Discover the secrets of how you can experience unlimited energy *now:*

- Learn how to operate your body at its very best.
- Master your own energy system.
- Resolve the emotions that drain you.
- Connect to your highest intelligence.
- Inspire yourself to connect more deeply to your infinite, eternal and unwavering support from your soul.

Banish the Blues
NOW
Catherine Carrigan

Banish the Blues NOW addresses:

HEALING DEPRESSION WITHOUT DRUGS using NATURAL HEALING remedies. Did you know that the Centers for Disease Control and Prevention reports that **11 percent of all Americans over the age of 12 take antidepressants**?

Women are more likely than men to take these drugs at every level of severity of depression.

Non-Hispanic white persons are more likely to take antidepressants than are non-Hispanic black and Mexican-American persons.

Of those **taking antidepressants, 60 percent have taken them for more than 2 years, and 14 percent have taken the drugs for more than 10 years.** About 8 percent of persons aged 12 and over with no current depressive symptoms took antidepressant medication.

Despite the widespread acceptance of natural healing methods, from 1988-1994 through 2005-2008, the rate of antidepressant use in the United States among all ages increased nearly 400 percent.

It is my prayer that my new book will be of service in teaching you how to heal depression without drugs, banishing your
blues FOR GOOD!

FOREWARD By Abram Hoffer, M.D., Ph.D., FRCP(C) Editor, *The Journal of Orthomolecular Medicine*

Unlimited Intuition
NOW
AMAZON
#1
BESTSELLER
Catherine Carrigan

READ *UNLIMITEDINTUITION NOW*
TO DEVELOP YOUR OWN PSYCHIC ABILITIES SO THAT YOU CAN RECEIVE GUIDANCE FROM YOUR SOUL.

How you will benefit:

- Pray to open your soul guidance.
- Learn how to read the energy in your. chakras with a pendulum
- Tune in to read your own body.
- Discover how to read the body of another person.
- Discern how much life force is in your food.
- Focus to tell if food is really good for your body.
- Practice how to muscle test yourself.
- Raise your vibration to listen to your angels.
- Get your ego out of the way so you can listen to divine guidance.
- Stay connected with loved ones when you are apart.
- Open your psychic centers of clairaudience, claircognizance, clairsentience and clairvoyance.
- Avoid other people's ego projections to see what's really going on.
- Protect your energy so you feel safe and grounded at all times and in all places.
- Stay out of trouble in dangerous situations.
- Understand how your different psychic gifts actually work.
- Deepen your connection to God and feel supported on all level

What is Social Media TODAY

Get Ready to Win
The Game of Social Media

Catherine Carrigan

What is Social Media Today
Where Social Media is Fun

Lose your fear of social media

Tackle Twitter

Make friends with Facebook

Become a Youtube superstar

Create compelling viral content

Grow and brand your business

Hit page one of Google

Build your audience

Increase your income

Develop raving fans

What is
Social Media Today

Hashtags, Keywords And You
Oh My!

Catherine Carrigan

Are you making mistakes that keep you broke, without customers, readers or the success you deserve?

Keywords and Hashtags are the foundation for successful social media marketing.

What is Social Media Today is a broad based social media marketing training program.

You will have a consistent social media presence and will be posting like an expert in no time.

Read this book to learn how to use keywords and hashtags to build your tribe online and draw more customers for your products, books, services and business.

The Little Book
of
Breathwork
Catherine Carrigan

The Little Book of BreathWork.

Stress reduction through breathing, affirmations and mudras.

The Little Book of BreathWork is a handbook you can use anytime, anywhere to lower your stress naturally.

What you will learn:

How to use breathing exercises to reduce high blood pressure, anxiety, depression, fatigue, insomnia, asthma, pain, sleep apnea and breathing problems.

Affirmations to uplift your soul.

Hand gestures called mudras you can use to increase your inner peace, emotional balance, creativity and grounding.

Author Catherine Carrigan has taught yoga and breath work for 24 years. In her work as a medical intuitive healer, she teaches people how to heal themselves naturally without drugs.

Made in the USA
Columbia, SC
14 January 2020

86590661R00136